Endorsements

Lynn Cowell has crafted my favorite kind of Bible study—practical, relatable, doable—wrapped around stories of women in Scripture. Her writing voice is warm and confident, and it's clear she's done her research, yet it never overshadows her enthusiasm for God's Word and how it can and will change our lives for the better.

—**Liz Curtis Higgs**, bestselling author of *Bad Girls of the Bible*

Like a snowflake in the palm of my hand, confidence seems to melt the moment I grasp it. One moment I'm buoyed with purpose and significance; the next I'm riddled with reminders of what I yet lack. My one comfort? God knows what I need, and He's promised to give it. If you need a confidence boost—one that won't evaporate in the heat of real life—join Lynn Cowell as she digs into biblical stories of women who discovered a God-delivered confidence they could count on. Always.

—**Michele Cushatt**, author of *I Am: A 60-Day Journey to Knowing Who You Are Because of Who He Is*

Do you sense God is calling you to take a step of faith and move outside your comfort zone? It might be a new job. Starting a Bible study. Ending a relationship. Opening a nonprofit. Going back to school. Adopting. You want to say yes, but you lack the confidence and courage to make that move. Through God's Word and personal stories, Lynn's book will help you identify your fears and insecurities and equip you with the courage and unshakable confidence you need to fulfill that call and reach your potential in Christ.

—**Wendy Blight**, member of Proverbs 31 First 5 Writing Team; author of *I Know His Name, Living So That,* and *Hidden Joy in a Dark Corner*

I long for studies that challenge me and help me walk out my faith. Lynn Cowell has accomplished that in *Fearless Women of the Bible*. It's fresh, interactive teaching. It feels like I'm sitting across from Lynn in a coffee shop, discovering how to depart from where I feel stuck to find deeper waters together. If you long to make your move, this is a book that will help you do just that.

—**Suzanne Eller**, bestselling author, blogger, international speaker, and Bible teacher

Self-doubt and insecurity have taken a toll on our lives for far too long. It's time to take back freedom and assurance that is ours in Christ, so that we can live in the fullness of God's purposes and plans. Don't let past failures, fear of future rejection, or everyday troubles hold you back any longer. Let Lynn Cowell show you how to boldly experience confident faith that will move you forward!

—**Renee Swope**, former Proverbs 31 Ministries radio cohost; bestselling author of *A Confident Heart*

Fearless Women of the Bible

Finding Unshakable Confidence Despite Your Fears and Failures

Lynn Cowell

H Harper*Christian* Resources

Fearless Women of the Bible
© 2022 by Lynn Cowell

Requests for information should be addressed to:
HarperChristian Resources, 3900 Sparks Dr. SE, Grand Rapids, Michigan 49546

Previously published as *Make Your Move* by Lynn Cowell (2017).

ISBN 978–0–310–14120–4 (softcover)
ISBN 978–0–310–14121–1 (ebook)

HarperChristian Resources titles may be purchased in bulk for church, business, fundraising, or ministry use. For information, please e-mail ResourceSpecialist@ChurchSource.com.

Published in association with the literary agency of FEDD Agency, Inc., Post Office Box 341973, Austin, TX 78734.

First Printing November 2022 / Printed in the United States of America

To Julie,

I've spent a lifetime watching you make
your move toward God despite your fears
and failures. What a beautiful thing it
has been, my friend. I love you!

Acknowledgments

The Lord has blessed me with so many wonderful people who have come alongside me:

Greg: God knew exactly who I would need to cheer for me on this adventure of writing and speaking. Thank you for doing that so well! I am very grateful, every day, to live this life of ours together. I love you!

Zach, Mariah, and Madi: My life is better being your mom. Thank you for every word you've read or I've made you listen to over the years. You've grown into amazing adults! I love our crazy, little family!

Robin Phillips: Thank you for seeing that God had a message for me to share and opening the doors for me to share it through HarperCollins Christian Publishing.

John Raymond and HarperCollins Christian Publishing: Thank you for holding this project together so that it didn't fall through the cracks. I am so grateful you have given me an opportunity to write for a new audience to empower women to find Christ Confidence. I so appreciate you!

Sara Riemersma: Every writer should have an editor like you, the kind who encourages them to dig deep and keep going but who also isn't afraid to say, "Try again." You are the best, my friend. I am so very, very grateful for you!

My Proverbs 31 Speaking and Writing Team: Ministry was never meant to be done alone, and I am thankful that the Lord chose you for me to minister with. I love us!

Lysa TerKeurst: Thank you for challenging us to not only know the Truth but also for living the Truth for our team to emulate. Your leadership is so dear to me!

Annette, Cindi, Danya, Jana, Kelly H., Kelly T., Rachel, Shelley, Stela: Thank you so much for being a part of my focus group. Your feedback made this study so much better. Thank you for pushing me!

Kaley Olsen: Thank you for bringing your brand of beautiful to help me share this message.

The Fedd Agency: I am so grateful for your help in finding new ways for me to share God's Word.

Contents

Introduction

I consider myself a pretty cool mom, but when my daughter, Madi, said she wanted to jump out of a plane together, I thought *no way*. She was thirteen years old when she started this concerning conversation: "Mom, for my eighteenth birthday, we're going skydiving." *Yeah, right!* I thought. I'm all about the experience and I love the outdoors. But there is a difference between exciting and absurd.

Not wanting to diminish her confidence, I joked with her for many years, trying to keep it light. To think that my girl wanted to do something so adventurous with her mom, of all people, was heartwarming. But deep down, I hoped she'd forget it and move on. The mere idea of floating in the open Carolina blue sky made me . . . well, let's not go there.

There is something you should know about me before we go any further. Sometimes, I can be all talk. Like the time I went on and on describing to my husband all we would see when we went snorkeling on a trip that he had won from his company. A girl from small-town Iowa, I grew up in the middle of seas of corn, not schools of fish. I knew nothing about the ocean. And it was obvious when I refused to leave the shore. The little mask sealing off the only airflow I had (or so it seemed) felt like a death trap. *Who in the world can possibly breathe this way?*

Heartbroken, I stood baking on the beach, as Greg called for me to come and see all God had created below the ocean's surface. I just couldn't. While my heart was floating next to him, immersing in cobalt blue, tangerine orange, and sunshine yellow sea life, my leaded feet were captive in the quicksand of the shore. I never found the courage to move.

You can understand then why I started freaking out as Madi's eighteenth birthday approached and she began reminding me of my promise. My girl really wanted to do this. All my bravado had gotten me in a whole lot of trouble!

So, I created a plan, a plan to get me out of this mess! I asked *her brother* to jump out of a plane with his sister in my place. When he agreed, my heart settled down. I could keep my promise. Well sort of . . . I paid for a promise. Now, I could look forward to the big weekend and to living vicariously through my kids. But when the day finally arrived, her brother couldn't come through!

Now what? The jump had been paid for. Two nonrefundable reservations confirmed. The hammering of my heart and moisture gathering on my palms reminded me that I couldn't let my daughter jump out of a plane alone. Someone had to jump.

Did that someone have to be me?

My guess is that you've never found yourself in a situation where you were pressured to free fall through the air. But maybe there has been a time when your life has felt like it was spiraling . . . and your confidence was falling with it.

The hot summer day when I drove with my family to the airfield was not the only time I've felt like I needed a grit I didn't have. Raising children whom I didn't always understand, overcoming rejections I couldn't avoid, and trusting God when my calling didn't make sense have all given me plenty of opportunities to lean into Jesus. I've needed to find a confidence that holds my head up when my heart is hanging low. The sort of confidence that doesn't slip away with each new obstacle and won't disintegrate when I need it most.

If you're anything like me, you're looking for the courage you need to make your move in spite of the fact that you sometimes feel fearful or possibly like a failure. Picking up this Bible study tells me you are looking for the source and how to tap into it.

That sweltering June day, I needed to jump out of a plane. Someone had to go with my girl and that someone needed to be me.

Sometimes, I think finding confidence means making a move even when, and most often when, you think you can't. I have found there are many people, including women in the Bible, who have needed confidence to act when they had none. Making their move was part of the process to finding God's confidence.

The sense of soaring while skydiving was both terrifying and thrilling, and it was one of the most exhilarating experiences in my life. I am so glad I jumped!

That leap would never have been possible had my body not been attached to the body of another that day. My jumper, the expert who had skydived thousands of times, knew exactly what he was doing. During the entire experience, he spoke directly in my ear, telling me exactly what to do next. His instructions made the jump safe and successful. As long as I was connected to my jumper, listening and obeying, the dive was amazing. But before I could dive, I had to willingly and intentionally secure myself to him.

Jesus is *our* jumper. Our first move in this journey of obtaining unshakable confidence is to secure ourselves to Jesus through His word, worship, and listening and talking to Him every day. This study will help you do just that!

Knowing I was dependent on the parachute above my head and the jumper attached to my back was unnerving yet comforting at the same time. I knew I was not alone and had all I needed for this amazing adventure.

I think that's what God wants us to experience with Him. The thrill of leaping into the great unknown, reaching our full potential in Him, fully equipped yet completely dependent. And that is done one small, brave jump at a time.

So, friends, let's do just that! God's Word will be our equipment and the Holy Spirit our expert jumper. Together, we will dive into God's Word and discover the women (and a few men as well) who found the power, confidence, and courage needed in God to do the work God called them to.

Fearless Women of the Bible can be read individually or with a small group. Small groups allow for deeper discussion as well as accountability and encouragement to draw closer in relationship with the Lord.

You will notice that I use different Bible translations throughout the study. I do so to bring variety and find deeper meaning in the text. No matter what translation you prefer, you will have no trouble using it for this study.

Fearless Women of the Bible will lead you through six chapters containing personal stories as well as the stories of women (and men) in the Bible who made courageous moves. Each chapter opens with a prayer and a memory verse. Begin your time with the Lord each day in prayer, inviting the Holy Spirit to bring His personal revelation to you through the study. The memory verse is provided so that you will carry God's word into your entire day. Type it into your phone; write it on a card. However you choose to memorize these verses, let's be intentional to write God's Word on our hearts.

Each lesson includes teaching, a section for Digging Deeper into the Bible, and a section to Apply It. Here is where you can write your own personal revelations that have come through the Scripture and study as well as thoughts you want to continue to reflect on. I also like to have a journal or notebook next to me because often I want more space for reflection or personal revelations I have had.

Friend, I have prayed for you and believe that God will reveal to you in a very personal way what He has for you in this study. You may find it written here in the words of this book or it may be a word He whispers to your heart. Let's get started, believing that together we will find His confidence to make our move and be fearless!

The Women of Exodus

WHEN CONFIDENCE FACES ADVERSITY

★

PRAYER: *Lord, I may be an ordinary, everyday, down-to-earth kind of woman, but I still want to make my move and find confidence in You. Encourage me through the study of the women of Exodus that women like me are exactly the type You love to use. Empower me, Holy Spirit. Arrest my fears so I can move forward. In Jesus' name, Amen.*

MEMORY VERSE: "For the LORD will be your confidence and will keep your foot from being caught."—Proverbs 3:26 (ESV)

DAY ONE

★

More Powerful Than Fear

HAVE YOU EVER NEEDED to do something but lacked the confidence or courage to do it? Go back to college? Give a presentation? Look for a new job? Move to a different city? I've so been there! Not just when it came to skydiving as I shared in the introduction, but also when it has come to pursuing my potential with God.

I think a part of us believes if *God* nudges us to do something, it won't be that hard. I'm just going to say that has not been *my* experience in this adventurous journey with Him.

Several years ago, one of my adventures began on the road to publishing. Not knowing just how hard the journey would be, I naively sent out my proposals. One by one, the replies filled my box, each one saying the same thing in a different way: *No.* It was as if a huge, rubber stamp marked REJECTION was stamped right across my forehead. The stamp got larger and ink darker with each notification.

No—You aren't well known. No—Your writing is not what we are looking for. No—We don't publish books for teens. I felt like my heart could not take another rejection.

Some days, I was brave. I gave myself a little pep talk, "Every no gets you closer to that yes." Other days, I curled up in a ball on my kitchen floor and wept. It all felt so very personal.

With no college degree, no background in English, and no platform as an author, I didn't offer a publisher the reasons to say yes that they were looking for. Encouragement from friends and family such as "God's timing is best" or "God will take care of it" were no longer working on my wounded heart. After five long years of noes, I received my nineteenth rejection letter. I wanted to quit. My confidence was shot. I felt like a complete failure.

Have you ever heard that you are not good enough over and over again? Are you in the middle of navigating rejection right now? Have you felt a rejection so deep it shook the very core of who you believed you were?

Maybe you can think of a time in your life when the enemy whispered the lie that you couldn't do it, whatever *it* was. You might be in that place today. You feel like you're not good enough. You're not fun enough. You don't have enough. You're not loved enough. Fear overshadows your confidence.

I wonder if these were some of the feelings of the women we'll meet this week: the women of the book of Exodus. They, too, may have believed they were not courageous enough. Not confident enough. Not brave enough for the task ahead.

And yet, we'll see by their courageous actions, what they may have felt and what they may have believed in the beginning all changed as they found the confidence they needed for the undertaking that lay before them.

I find it so very exciting that this story of women that took place long ago in an ancient land can be exactly what you and I need today to empower us with confidence. Exodus comes from a Greek word *exodos plithous* meaning "departure." It is the narrative of the deliverance of the children of Israel from slavery in Egypt and their journey toward God's Promised Land of Canaan. Moses, who is believed to have been the author, served as the Israelites' imperfect leader. For years, the Israelites had been able to put their trust and welfare in the hands of the Egyptian Pharaoh. When a new Pharaoh came into power, all that security was stripped away. Completely out of control, they needed a strength and confidence to navigate this new and challenging change.

Maybe you know that feeling. Just when it seemed life had calmed down and you were enjoying a season of serenity, your peace was pulled out from under you. With circumstances spinning out of your control, you were left staring at a choice. Spin out of control with them or turn to the Lord for the strength and courage to face your situation.

Digging Deeper

Please read Exodus 1:8–21 for the foundation for today's study. Write any details that stand out to you below.

_____

_____

_____

Paranoia whispers to Pharaoh that if Egypt went to war, the Hebrews would side with the enemy, fighting against Egypt and leaving the land. A cold sweat beads up on his forehead just thinking of so many people against him, so Pharaoh devises an evil scheme to combat his building anxiety. First, slave labor. And still the people multiply. So next he determines to stop the Hebrew nation from growing by killing all the newborn Hebrew male babies.

Describe a time when, like the Hebrews, others turned against you and you did nothing to deserve it. As you look back at that situation, how did that experience impact your confidence?

_____

_____

_____

Pharaoh was fear-filled, but he had reason for concern. When the sons of Jacob came from Canaan to Egypt, they came as a clan of seventy. Now they have increased to number two million (Exodus 1:1–7).

According to Genesis 22:17–18, what had God promised the Israelites as far as their future was concerned?

_____

_____

_____

Maybe Pharaoh knew of this promise that the Israelite God had made to them. Seeing just how blessed they were, his fear-induced instincts told him he had to bring an end to their prosperity. His plan: intimidation, aimed at two Hebrew women. Meet Shiphrah and Puah.

According to Exodus 1:11–14, how effective was Pharaoh's first attempt to oppress and brutalize the Hebrews to cease their growth?

_____

_____

_____

_____

According to Exodus 1:15–16, why did Pharaoh pick these two women to carry out his dirty work? Have you ever been in a situation when you were asked to do something illegal or unethical? How did you respond?

_____

_____

_____

_____

_____

The monarch delivers this edict to the midwives: Kill your own people. "When you are helping the Hebrew women during childbirth on the delivery stool, if you see that the baby is a boy, kill him; but if it is a girl, let her live" (Exodus 1:16).

From that day forward, life could not go on as usual for Shiphrah and Puah, who once delighted in bringing God's babies into the world. A choice had to be made. They needed to make up their minds what move they would make *before* they received their next patient's call.

Fear would drive their response. The question—what kind of fear? *Whom* would they fear? Exodus 1:17 supplies our answer: "The midwives, however, feared God and did not do what the king of Egypt had told them to do; they let the boys live."

The word translated *fear* in verse 17 is quite different from the type of fear Shiphrah and Puah may have had toward Pharaoh. This fear is the Hebrew word *yare*: to be afraid, be frightened, to revere, to respect or to be awesome.[1] It is a fear that comes from a combination of love, hope, and reverence, not extreme apprehension.

How does fearing God, having a deep reverence for Him, and having courage fit together in the lives of these women?

_____

_____

_____

Has there been a time in your life when the fear of God—your desire to honor Him because you love Him—empowered you to be courageous? Or can you picture yourself in a scenario where this might happen?

As a teenager, I often bypassed situations where I had the opportunity to have fun if it brought the possibility of getting into trouble. My mind often went to the possible ramifications of my choices. A high school party with alcohol? *What if someone called the police?* Making out with a guy? *What if we got caught?* Some of my friends thought my straight-and-narrow living simply came from my rock-solid faith. Honestly, the fear of God had much more to do with it. I was just plain afraid to go against Him. As a young person, sometimes this tender conscience drove me crazy. I just couldn't get wild like my friends, and sometimes it was maddening. (I am confident the prayers of my mother had a great deal to do with it!) As my relationship with the Lord developed and my love for Him grew, the desire to please Him grew from a negative type of fear into a healthy fear—a desire to want to please Him because I love Him. This desire to show Him I love Him compels me to obedience.

> ## My desire to show Christ I love Him compels me to obedience.

When Pharaoh's attempt to stifle Hebrew prosperity through slave labor failed, he moved on to Plan B (directing the midwives to kill every newborn Hebrew male). When that didn't work, Pharaoh summoned Shiphrah and Puah to his throne. They had not been following the command he had given them to kill the Hebrew males as they were born and now they were being called to account for their actions. I've never been summoned by the head of a country. The closest I've come is being called into the office of someone in authority over me. Whenever that has happened, I have immediately panicked. My mind turns to fear first. *What did I do? Why is she calling?*

Shiphrah and Puah had every reason to be terrified when they received the command to come to Pharaoh's throne. This ruler of Egypt was ruthless. They had, at worst, disobeyed him; at best, disappointed him to a fault.

Though Shiphrah and Puah may have been trembling in Pharaoh's presence, they did not allow the situation to paralyze them. Yes, they were struck with awe but not by the powerful, intimidation of Pharaoh. Their fear, directed toward the majesty of their God, empowered them with the courage to let the male sons live, and that courage would not fail them now as they faced accounting for their actions.

Pharaoh's pressure brought forth an effect for sure, but it was the opposite of what he intended. Pharaoh's edict brought out, from a place deep within, a faith deeper than the women's fear of his earthly power. Shiphrah and Puah's faith in God compelled them toward courage. The God of Abraham, Isaac, and Jacob, who had brought the Israelites safely to Egypt in the famine, would not quit on His plan to make Israel a great nation.

Shiphrah and Puah chose to fear God over fearing Pharaoh.

Do it scared became their motto.

God would come through just as Hebrews 6:10 says: "God is not unjust; he will not forget your work and the love you have shown him as you have helped his people and continue to help them."

Shiphrah and Puah chose to be courageous not because they were fearless. They chose to be brave because their love for their God was stronger than their fear of a human. God's love for them empowered them and helped them move forward.

Apply It

Describe an area in your life that is causing you fear now or has caused you fear in your past.

_____

_____

_____

Just as a fear of Pharaoh's power and punishment may have pressed on Shiphrah and Puah, this same type of fear presses on us too. It tries to tell us what to do, when, and how to do it. *Text her. Do it now. Speak your mind. Don't let them push you around.* Like a miniature dictator, fear from the enemy attempts to call the shots.

Today, tune in to when this fear is trying to speak to you. Ask the Lord to set off an alarm in your mind, alerting you to when fear's voice is attempting to dictate your actions. When you feel fear trying to pull you under, speak this week's memory verse over your heart: "For the LORD will be your confidence and will keep your foot from being caught" (Proverbs 3:26 ESV).

Let's end with a prayer today:

Father, I'm tired of this unhealthy fear pushing me around. We know that fear is not from you because, "There is no fear in love. But perfect love drives out fear, because fear has to do with punishment. The one who fears is not made perfect in love" (1 John 4:18). Drive fear from me with Your love today. In Jesus' name, Amen.

★

Do It Scared

MEMORY VERSE: "For the LORD will be your confidence and will keep your foot from being caught."—Proverbs 3:26 (ESV)

DURING HER SENIOR YEAR of high school, my youngest daughter, Madi, started traveling with me whenever I spoke. Often, at the end of the conferences, we would do a question and answer time with girls and their moms. When speaking, Madi would light up. Her passion to encourage young women to fully pursue Christ could not be contained.

Yet, after we had partnered together a few times, Madi informed me that although she had considered it, she could never become a speaker. "Why? You seem so natural," I wanted to know.

"Every time I get ready to speak, I get so scared! Whether I'm with you on a stage or in a classroom at school, I feel like I can't do it." Boy, did I know what she was talking about!

Even after speaking for many years, I still have to "do it scared." I have to look to Jesus to find the courage to make my move to share His word with others. Right before I get ready to speak, it's as if my mind and body conspire to hold me down. *You really have to go to the bathroom!* "*Do you even remember your opening story?*" "*What if someone falls asleep in the middle of your message?*" As these fears surface— fears all based on things that have happened to me before—I have to remind myself, *God has called me to this assignment. He will empower me to complete it.* I have to remind myself to fear God more than I fear the people I'm speaking to.

I used to think that if I felt afraid, that was an indication that what I was about to do wasn't from God. I've learned that is just not the case. This is not the kind of fear protecting us from danger; our fear has a different source. We may fear failure or looking like a fool. Often, the discomfort of doing something we have never done tries to lock us down before we even get started.

Digging Deeper

Read Acts 4:18–22 and Acts 5:27–29. Peter ran into multiple situations that were also very scary. What was his response in both of these passages?

_____

_____

_____

> ## Being afraid doesn't mean
> ## it's not from God.

Courage is not a feeling. Courage is a noun, the strength to go forward *even* in the face of fear.

One of the Hebrew words for *courage* is *ruah*, which can mean "breath of God" and can be used to describe God's creative activity.[2] Just as He did in Genesis 1, God is creating something out of nothing in you and me. Alone, we don't possess confidence, courage, or bravery. He is forming this fortitude where there has been a void, where it never has existed before. He is very good at making something out of nothing.

Psalm 33:6–9 tells us, "By the word of the LORD the heavens were made, their starry host by the breath of his mouth. He gathers the waters of the sea into jars; he puts the deep into storehouses. Let all the earth fear the LORD; let all the people of the world revere him. For he spoke, and it came to be; he commanded, and it stood firm."

According to Genesis 1 and Psalm 33:6–9, what does God use to create something out of nothing?

_____

_____

From these verses, what can we learn about the power of words?

_____

_____

_____

_____

All God has to do is speak and it is done! By *His* word, we are empowered. We can believe that the power that brought the sun shining through your window and the moon lighting up the night sky and that raised Jesus Christ from the dead is the same power that can bring the confidence we need to do all He calls us to do. God gave Shiphrah and Puah the confidence they needed to deny Pharaoh and obey God. He will give us His confidence as well.

Minds made up, the women move forward, determined to obey God rather than Pharaoh. At any moment, the moaning of a mother and the cries of a newborn could deliver an Egyptian henchman to the delivery door. The women's brave steps would not be a once-and-done move. They would need to bring forth courage *each time* a Hebrew sister's delivery time had come. The mother in labor and the midwives would have to be brave together. The nation of Israel depended on it.

When have you or when could you partner with another sister in the Lord to make a move of courage, big or small?

_____

_____

_____

What difference can it make having another beside you?

_____

_____

_____

We live in a culture that is more connected than ever before through social media. Yet studies show we are a culture that is also lonelier than ever before. It is killing us. Literally. "The subjective feeling of loneliness increases risk of death by 26%, according to the new study in the journal *Perspectives on Psychological Science*. Social isolation—or lacking social connection—and living alone were found to be even more devastating to a person's health than feeling lonely, respectively increasing mortality risk by 29% and 32%."[3]

Yes, we need to be confident and courageous, and we are more confident and more courageous together. I have found this to be so true in my life. Surrounding myself with others who are also moving forward in their faith encourages me each day to keep moving in God's direction.

How important were the rebellious and obedient acts of Shiphrah and Puah for the Israelite people? What might have been the effects if they had chosen to fear Pharaoh over God?

_____

_____

_____

_____

If Shiphrah and Puah had not feared God more than they feared man, Israel as a nation could have died out. Pharaoh's diabolical plan would have succeeded. This nation, on the cusp of a new birth, would have been buried but for two women. God entrusted two ordinary women because they honored, respected, and revered Him. Every time they empowered a child to continue to breathe life, the very breath God had given, they honored God's greatness.

"For the foolishness of God is wiser than human wisdom, and the weakness of God is stronger than human strength" (1 Corinthians 1:25).

The budding Israelite nation was continuing to grow and it didn't go unnoticed by Pharaoh. Maybe as they worked side by side, waiting for Hebrew babies to enter the world, Shiphrah and Puah processed the answer they would surely have to give for their daring acts. Possibly, they put themselves in a "worst case scenario."

I still have some work to do when it comes to this type of preparation. I put off thinking through the plans I will need to have in place should the "worst case scenario" come to pass.

➤ Backing up my computer in case it breaks.

➤ Filling up my spare tire in case of a flat.

➤ Printing pictures off my phone before it dies.

All good and wise actions require plans that I all too often fail to execute.

But the worst case did come to pass for these women. And they were ready.

First Peter 3:15 tells us we should also be ready. Ready for what exactly?

_____

_____

_____

The day had finally come and it was none too soon. My husband and I had stalled on making needed repairs to our backyard, and I was happy to finally see the repair crew arrive. As the workers sweated away outside, I typed away in my office. Finishing my article, I ended my writing with this challenge: "Today, let's you and I look for someone who needs our prayers."

Sounds good, doesn't it?

Looking out in the yard, I noticed a new worker, so I headed out to introduce myself.

After exchanging greetings, it didn't take long to learn that Johnny was fairly new to our community. We swapped stories of how we both had to make adjustments when we moved from our home states to the South, but now we both loved it. Then that nagging, *I've got to get back to work* feeling crept in my mind. Yet as I tried to figure out how to get back to my work, I felt a nudge from the Holy Spirit in my heart.

What is most important is the person in front of you.

I paid attention to the prompting and continued listening to Johnny before heading inside to grab my checkbook. As I began writing the check for the payment, I noticed the name of our church on my pen.

Ask Johnny to church, came the second nudge. Honestly, this one scared me. I told myself, *"I'll ask Johnny to church if I see him again."*

I wrote the check and looked again into my backyard. No Johnny. Will you judge me if I tell you I felt relief? *I don't have to do the hard thing,* I thought. Then, I turned around, only to spot Johnny's truck through the front window. He *was* still at our home.

Ask Johnny to church, I sensed the Holy Spirit say again.

I needed to obey.

How am I going to do this, Lord? It's so unnatural. Then, I had the idea: Go get the mail and start a conversation. Trying to dig up a courage I didn't feel, I headed down our driveway. After checking the mailbox, I stopped by Johnny's truck.

Honestly, I was terrified to even start dialoging again. With my heart pounding and with the Lord's help, I asked Johnny if he had found a church yet. As I blurted out my question, I stuck out my church's pen. Johnny looked at the pen. He looked at me. Then, as a dam breaking from flood waters, he poured out his heart. Hurt by a relationship in his prior church, Johnny desperately wanted to believe that God was still good. He had been searching for a way to reconnect with God again.

I was stunned. To think I had almost missed this opportunity because I didn't want to do it scared. After a few minutes, I attempted to wrap up our conversation, when I sensed God wasn't finished yet.

That nudging in my heart came again. *You have yet to pray for Johnny.*

Oh man! I really thought I had done what God wanted me to do, but apparently I wasn't done yet. My mind quickly gathered together so many reasons for not praying with Johnny right then and there. *I'm in the middle of my cul-de-sac. My neighbors might see me. They could draw a wrongful conclusion.*

None of my excuses caused the prompting to fade. Instead, I sensed God's peace; He could take care of each and every concern.

So, I said five simple words to Johnny: "Can I pray for you?"

As I prayed for this man in the middle of my cul-de-sac, God made His presence known. You don't need a church to have church! And as I walked back up my driveway, my heart was doing flip-flops again. Not because I was scared, but because of the joy I found in obeying.

Just because we feel afraid to do what we feel prompted to do doesn't mean it's not God asking. Courage is not a feeling; it's the strength to move *even* in the face of fear.

Apply It

Maybe like me, one of the areas where you want to become fearless is finding the boldness to share your faith. You want to share Jesus and not let what others think hold you back. You desire the courage to *do it afraid* and allow the fear of God to compel you more than your fear of people.

We can be assured: God wants us to fear Him more than we fear anything else. Let's start overcoming our fear of people by fanning our fear of God. I am challenged today to be on the lookout for ways He is encouraging me to share Him with others. Join me in simply looking for someone who needs prayer. Boldly ask another: "How can I pray for you today?"

★

God Can Use Anyone

MEMORY VERSE: "For the LORD will be your confidence and will keep your foot from being caught."—Proverbs 3:26 (ESV)

WHEN YOU'RE A GIRL LIKE ME, without a college degree, seeing God use ordinary people increases my faith and confidence that He can use me, too!

In 2014, I was introduced to a young girl named Katie Davis, via her book, *Kisses from Katie.*

Disobeying and disappointing her parents by forgoing college, plus breaking up with the love of her life, Katie followed Jesus by going on a short-term mission trip to Uganda. Then the eighteen-year-old senior class president and homecoming queen stayed in Africa, and subsequently *adopted* thirteen children and established a ministry, Amazima, that feeds and sends hundreds more to school while teaching them the Word of God.

Through her book, Katie challenged me to look for ways to keep saying yes to the people God places in front of me, to change the world one person at a time. That process begins when we believe God can use anyone, whether that's an eighteen-year-old girl or even me! The women of Exodus encourage us in this truth.

Pharaoh's ambition was clear: Stop the blessings God was pouring out on His children. Genocide would be his vehicle. In Pharaoh's eyes, the increase of God's favor on the nation of Israel equaled a threat to his own. God, however, would not stand idly by and watch His children suffer. He sent help just as He later promised in 1 Samuel 2:9: "He will guard the feet of his faithful servants, but the wicked will be silenced in the place of darkness. 'It is not by strength that one prevails.'"

Shiphrah and Puah would not be the only women in the tale of the exodus of Israel who would need God's confidence and the bravery to do it scared.

Digging Deeper

Read Exodus 2:1–10. If you are familiar with this story, use an online Bible and read this in a version other than your normal study Bible. My mind grows familiar with the Bible that I study from daily. Reading in another version allows me to see things I might have missed before.

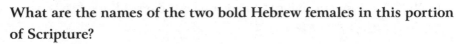

What are the names of the two bold Hebrew females in this portion of Scripture?

_____

_____

Trick question! They are not mentioned by name.

We learn later in Exodus 6:20 that the mother of Moses was Jochebed. We are given no other details in Exodus 2 of this rock-of-a-woman except that she was a Levite who married a man of the house of Levi (2:1).

Yet Jochebed, whose name implies "glory of Jehovah" or "Jehovah (is her or our) glory" is a key piece of God's plan to bring salvation to His people. Jochebed would have a total of three children—all three pivotal persons in the redemption of the Israelites from Egyptian bondage.[4]

Moses, although her youngest, was her most well-known child.

Read: Exodus 33:11; Numbers 12:3; and Deuteronomy 34:5–6.

What does Scripture tell us is unique about Moses and his relationship with God?

_____

_____

_____

From adopted child to shepherd to redeemer of thousands, we could argue that Moses was one of the greatest leaders to ever live. In the world's estimation, he was a man who went from nothing to something.

Jochebed's second child, Aaron, was the first high priest of the Israelites. God not only called Aaron to this important role, but Aaron's entire lineage would become Israel's priests.

According to Exodus 28:29–30, what service of honor was Aaron given as the high priest?

_____

_____

_____

Aaron was also used as God's mouthpiece for Moses when Moses would deliver God's message of deliverance to Pharaoh (Exodus 4:14–16).

The oldest child of this ordinary woman was the spunky little thing who followed her brother's boat in the Nile. Described as "his sister" in Exodus 2:4, the girl we later come to know as Miriam is brave beyond her years. It is as if she already knew what Paul would write one day,

"Don't let anyone look down on you because you are young, but set an example for the believers in speech, in conduct, in love, in faith and in purity" (1 Timothy 4:12).

She certainly set an example as she headed to the water. There is no evidence that Miriam went to the bank of the Nile at the command of her mother.

What title does Exodus 15:20 give Miriam?

_____

_____

How could her gift have played into what took place the day she went down to the Nile River to watch over her brother?

_____

_____

Maybe, like Jochebed, Miriam had also seen that Moses "was a fine child" (Exodus 2:2) and somehow sensed that he was a vital part of God's plan for redemption for the Israelites.

In what ways might God speak to us today? Describe a time when you had an instinct or feeling that something was about to happen.

_____

_____

_____

_____

How did that sense impact the way you acted on that day?

_____

_____

_____

_____

_____

Unlike many of us, this young girl doesn't care what others think of her actions because she's standing for what's right. She is audacious and gutsy enough to not only speak to Pharaoh's daughter but to offer the princess advice! Wise beyond her years, she concocts a plan to get her mother involved in the raising of her brother in his early years *and* to have Jochebed paid for it as well.

Miriam not only stands by her brother at this critical time but also comes alongside Moses later in his life during the exodus of God's people. Using her gifts of music and poetry, Miriam helps God's people worship Him in the desert. Exodus 15 records the song Miriam led the Israelites in. I, too, sang these words, in our church as a young girl: "I will sing unto the LORD, for he hath triumphed gloriously: the horse and his rider hath he thrown into the sea. The LORD is my strength and song, and he is become my salvation: he is my God, and I will prepare him an habitation; my father's God, and I will exalt him" (Exodus 15:1b–2 KJV). A song makes Scripture stick like nothing else.

Three ordinary children grew up to become three extraordinary adults. I find so much hope in the mothering role of Jochebed. While she lived a life of boldly trusting God, her children were watching every step. She may not have been aware of how her actions were impacting them. She could not have known what type of adults they would become. God did. He was preparing them to have great influence with a willingness to "do it afraid."

Confidence was not something Jochebed's children were born with; it was some *One* they conformed *to*. The more they came to know the God of Jochebed, their fear of God grew.

> *Confidence was not something they were born with; it was some One they conformed to.*

Shiphrah, Puah, Jochebed, and Miriam—all ordinary women—all used in extraordinary ways by God.

Ordinary women like you and me, who stood up to a king, who were bold enough to defy human authority in order to obey the Authority over all.

They were women who took risks that could have led to their own deaths, so that another might live. Women who valued others above themselves.

They challenge me to choose the steps I take based on what God can do in me and through me, rather than based on the comfort I crave. Their stories provoke me to do what *I* can to help others and be a part of change in my community, in my church, and in my country.

Read Acts 5:29–40 to learn of someone who stood up to those with religious authority. Verse 34 tells us who he is. What was his name? Who was he standing up to?

_____

_____

_____

God can fill our mouth with words to move people. In Acts 5:34, God used an educated man speaking to educated people, but his words were ones they did not want to hear. The Holy Spirit empowered him to speak words that "persuaded" them to go in a completely different direction.

In Acts 4, Peter and John also stood up to the religious authorities. What adjective is used to describe Peter and John in verse 13?

_____

_____

Peter, previously known as a coward, shows tremendous courage, boldly making known the name and power of Jesus of Nazareth to those who have a history of killing those so bold.

Who does Acts 4:8 give credit to for Peter's newfound courage?

_____

_____

Jesus can and wants to use us all. Educated or uneducated. With an important job or an ordinary one. Famous or unknown. As His Holy Spirit fills us, He develops in us the courage and confidence we need to do the work He gives us to do, including sharing Christ's offer of salvation with others.

Apply It

God also is challenging you and me to boldly move forward in His power.

You may not be asked to speak up to your nation's leader, but God may be calling you to be brave enough to speak up to your boss, your coworker, your neighbor, or a friend. You may see practices at your workplace that are unethical or illegal, and you are the voice God wants to use for correction. He can give you the bravery you need to confront that situation.

You may be the bold voice that brings the gospel to your family. Perhaps you've been silenced. The Lord is calling you and me to be bold, to live out our faith in our deeds and actions. You might be the voice of change in your own community, church, and country, one who will no longer sit by and simply watch as others are oppressed and pushed down by culture.

God has given us much and He calls us to move, to take action.

What is one step of courage, big or small, that you can take?

_____

_____

Today He says to you, "Fear not, for I am with you; be not dismayed, for I am your God; I will strengthen you, I will help you, I will uphold you with my righteous right hand" (Isaiah 41:10 ESV).

Lord, reading the stories of these women gives me courage, but it is easy to be courageous as I sit here. What I need is an opportunity to put this truth into practice. I need a fearlessness that moves forward when confronted. Holy Spirit, please cause my ears and eyes to be open and look for these opportunities. Speak to me. Help me to make my move. In Jesus' name, Amen.

★

Contagious Courage

MEMORY VERSE: "For the LORD will be your confidence and will keep your foot from being caught."—Proverbs 3:26 (ESV)

EACH DAY I STARTED MY WORKDAY by telling myself, *You can do this! It's not a big deal.* For many people, the task I needed to complete would be effortless. But not me.

Even though writing this study would help others, that motivation wasn't enough to push me through. The fear of failure crippled me. I finally found the courage I needed to push past my phobia when Shiphrah and Puah's story leapt off the page and into my heart.

I saw for the first time that the first two chapters of Exodus tell the tale of a chain of courage—one act of fearlessness prompting another until the whole of these women's actions changed history. Like these women, God is calling you and me to be a part of contagious courage.

Digging Deeper

Reread Exodus 1:15–Exodus 2:10, seeing this piece of history as a whole.

If this passage were a play, *Contagious Courage*, it might look something like this:

Act 1: Shiphrah and Puah are commanded by Pharaoh to kill all males as soon as they are born. The brave women obey God rather than Pharaoh in a courageous act of rebellion against the king.

Act 2: Shiphrah, Puah, and Moses's mother, Jochebed (between her labor pains) discuss their options should this third child be a boy. In hushed tones they huddle, piecing together a plan for his survival. How would Jochebed answer questions about her delivery? Disguise her newly changed body? Where could they put the baby as he grew? How long could they keep him quiet?

As they make their plans, they rehearse their history with God. He had proven to the Hebrews that He could and would care for them, even in this foreign country. Their confidence in the one true God grows and their fear of their fierce enemy wanes as they move forward. Cowardice gives way to courage when we rehearse the faithfulness of God.

> ## Cowardice gives way to courage when we rehearse the faithfulness of God.

Once Moses is born, rather than killing her son, Jochebed courageously hides him at home. When she can no longer keep his existence a secret, she puts her son in a basket among the tall reeds of the Nile River. She is one fearless woman!

Act 3: Moses's sister Miriam stands by, watching the basket boat float on the Nile. But she isn't just observing. When Pharaoh's daughter calls for the basket to be brought to her, this girl-with-grit steps up and addresses the princess, giving royalty advice on how the child can be cared for.

Do you see the chain reaction one woman's courage had on another? Shiphrah and Puah decide to defy Pharaoh.

Jochebed, in a similar move, chooses courage instead of compromise. Miriam, inspired by her mother, moves fearlessly toward the princess.

A ripple effect can take place when one person takes a daring step and others witness it. News of the righteous rebellion of Shiphrah and Puah would have traveled through the whole community, reaching the ears of Jochebed. Miriam would have witnessed her mother's fearlessness each day she cared for baby Moses.

Can you think of a time when you were witness to someone's step of faith? What impact did this act have on you?

_____

_____

_____

_____

_____

Just as Shiphrah and Puah didn't know if they might be executed for not murdering Hebrew babies, Jochebed would not have known what would be the outcome of her audacious act. *Would she be found out and punished? Would her choice bring danger on her husband and her two other children? Was it irresponsible to risk all of their lives for one? Would the little vessel hold up once Moses was put in it? Would a wild animal find it?*

Jochebed followed her heroic instincts without any guarantees that any of her plan would work.

None of the women knew the future blessing resulting from her obedience to God.

According to Exodus 1:20–21, what was the result of the midwives' obedience for the Israelites?

_____

_____

What was the result of the midwives' obedience personally?

_____

_____

According to Exodus 2:9, what reward was given to Miriam and Jochebed for their bravery?

_____

_____

_____

_____

I want to be part of a chain of courage too!

As a young mother, my mom stepped out of her social norm, embraced Jesus as her Savior, and became a prayer warrior for her eight children. Even though several were already adults when she came to know Christ, through her prayers and life testimony, all of us serve Him today.

Seeing my mother's fearless faith gives me courage to make a difference in my world. Seeing God answer her prayers for her children empowers me to pray for my children's relationship with the Lord, asking God that they will follow the steps of Miriam. My desire is for them to be on the lookout for where God can use them—and when the time is right, boldly step up with the wisdom God gives them.

What if the midwives were not courageous in defying Pharaoh's edict? Moses's mother Jochebed would not have had the opportunity to hide her baby boy in the Nile. Moses would have been dead. End of story.

If Jochebed had not courageously hid Moses, Miriam would not have been bold enough to speak to Pharaoh's daughter. There would have been no need for her to stand on the shores of the Nile, no reason for her to step out.

If Miriam had not been courageous and spoken to Pharaoh's daughter . . . who knows what would have happened to the millions of Israelites Moses led out of slavery.

But they were courageous.

They took steps of bravery, making it possible for the next woman to be brave. Maybe you remember a lesson from science class: Newton's first law of motion. It says: An object at rest stays at rest and an object in motion stays in motion with the same speed and in the same direction unless acted upon by an unbalanced force.[5]

I love how God's word was proving itself true before Newton ever came up with his law. Shiphrah and Puah set the movement of faith into motion. They went against the grain, against the ungodly command of the government, in order to move toward God. News traveled; others heard of their bravery. This motion pushed other women in their community to move in the same direction: obeying God rather than men. Their courage changed the course of Jochebed and Miriam and who knows how many other women who are not listed here in Scripture. They gave other women the permission to be brave and, in doing so, Shiphrah and Puah changed the course of history!

One woman's courageous act opens the door of courage for another.

> ## One woman's courageous act opens the door of courage for another.

I've been pondering this chain reaction and thinking of so many women throughout history whose courage opened the door for others.

Harriet Tubman (interestingly called "Moses") led approximately seventy slaves and their families to freedom during the Civil War and became the first woman to lead an armed expedition. Her name was feared by slave owners because of her courage.[6]

Women like Harriet Tubman, who were a part of the abolition movement, sparked the suffrage movement for women's right to vote and own property. These champions of courage paved the way for women in America to be able to vote in each election.

Catherine Booth, cofounder of the Salvation Army, led the way for women to be able to publicly share the gospel. Her acts of bravery opened doors for women coming behind her to be able to live out the calling of God on their lives. Catherine Booth opened the door for me and for you to share the Word of God aloud. She stood up to religious authority, who felt women were not to speak up. She boldly spoke what she felt God's Word said.[7]

I could go on and on, telling of the courageous women who have gone before us, opening doors so that we can have the opportunity to be brave and make a difference in our world at our time.

For many of these women, their steps of courage were ones taken over and over again. Harriet Tubman made some thirteen freedom trips during the course of the four-year Civil War. Catherine Booth spent more than twenty years defending the right of women to be able to preach the gospel, having to overcome significant timidity to do so.

Likewise, who knows how long Shiphrah and Puah allowed illegal births or how many close calls Jochebed had hiding the infant Moses?

Obeying God often requires us to persevere undaunted. When the answers and change don't come quickly, we need not be dismayed or discouraged. Galatians 6:9 says, "Let us not become weary in doing good, for at the proper time we will reap a harvest if we do not give up." God's Word says, we *will*, not we *might*. The Lord can empower us with great courage even when our confidence is stretched again and again. Rehearsing His faithfulness causes our courage to arise. Then we are enabled and empowered to open the doors of courage for those coming after us.

Apply It

How about you? How will you move toward courage like the women who have gone before you?

Is God calling you to be the first in your family to break out? To step up and bravely make decisions to bring God's redemption to your family line? To redefine "normal" in your family's legacy?

Maybe like me, you are blessed to have witnessed the courage of another, and it's empowered you toward bravery. We have to be careful to not become complacent or comfortable.

Where will you invest in another to keep the chain of courage going? We can start by:

➤ Praying for courage. We can bravely ask the Lord to put us in situations that require us to be courageous for Him, then be on the lookout for these opportunities each day.

➤ Surrounding ourselves with others who are courageous. We become like those with whom we spend time. Are there people in our lives who are taking risks with God? If not, we need to find courageous people and spend time with them.

➤ Reading stories of others (in the Bible or other books) who've been courageous. Proverbs 4:23 tells us, "Above all else, guard your heart, for everything you do flows from it." *Everything you do.* Since *everything we do* flows from our heart, let's intentionally fill it with courage and bravery so that we will do what is courageous and brave!

➤ Making our move to bring courage to another person who needs bravery too!

Lord, help us to choose courage over fear. We need the Holy Spirit to empower us to lean on You and make the moves You call us to take. In Jesus' name, Amen.

★

The Soil Confidence Grows In

MEMORY VERSE: "For the Lord will be your confidence and will keep your foot from being caught."—Proverbs 3:26 (ESV)

SITTING ON BLANKETS at a flag football game, the moms around me shared their concerns about their older children. Their sons playing football that day were their youngest, while our son was our oldest. Having children entering high school, they talked about the trials their kids would soon navigate.

Under my breath, I whispered to myself, "Being a Christian in high school was so hard!" One of the moms quickly picked up on my comment. "You were a Christian in high school?" My affirmative response was not all that amazing to me. Next thing I knew, the moms were asking me to mentor their daughters. "I don't think so," was my quick reply. *What did I know about teens?* My kids were nine, six, and three years old. We hadn't learned how to navigate teen waters yet, nor did I feel equipped to wade into them. It was not a place I was eager to go.

The next morning in church, I stood with my hands raised high, worshiping my Lord. With my eyes shut, a picture of sorts entered my mind. I was sitting in my backyard, surrounded by a small group of teen girls. Eating pizza together, I was sharing with them my story of running after God in high school. *Oh no! What could this mean?* I was afraid it meant what I thought it meant.

After church, I shared my "picture" with my husband. "Sounds like God to me, Lynn. You had better do it." But I didn't want to! I *did* want to obey God. More than anything in my life, I feared God. Out of respect and awe for Him, as well as His place of authority, I wanted Him to always make the last call in my life. So, reluctantly and before I could talk myself out of it, I invited a group of girls over. Just like the picture, I did what I felt God was calling me to do: I ordered pizza and shared my story.

Remember how I said I used to think that if God asked you to do something, the least He could do was not make it difficult? That was not my experience that night either.

Interruptions, one after another, chopped into our time. These were not normal interruptions. The first call came from my sister-in-law; there had been a shooting in their neighborhood. She wanted her girl to be careful coming home. Another mom called to say her daughter's pet toucan that had flown away returned. Another mom locked her keys out of her car and needed her daughter's help. I am sure the girls could sense my frustration of wasting my time, energy, and money.

Can I just be honest and tell you I was so mad at God? I had obeyed, did what I felt He wanted me to do. I had been afraid. *What would these teen girls think of this mom who wanted to hang out with them*? I had done it afraid . . . and it had not turned out. *Thanks for nothing* crossed my mind as I wrapped up the night, quickly shoving pizza boxes in the garbage.

One neighbor girl lingered. After helping me clean up, she asked, "Would you mentor me?"

Would you hate me if I told you I said no? That night, I was so fed up with the situation. If that experience was any indication of what it meant to mentor teens, my answer was *"Thanks, but no thanks!"* My confidence in this stepping out for God was gone.

I knew there was a group of Christian teens at her high school she could join. That was not what she wanted, she said. She wanted a mentor.

I told her I would give her a chance, but if she wasn't serious, I would be done. (I am so embarrassed! How mean of me!)

You know, that night in my backyard, I didn't go into it with any preconceived notions about the future. I hadn't any thoughts of "what this meant" or why God was asking me to do this or what it was for. I didn't dream of growing a small group, writing Bible studies, or traveling the country speaking at events. What I did know was there was a nudging in my heart that I believe came from God. And if God was asking me to do something, I was going to do it. No matter how small it was or how big. No matter what, I would obey Him.

God wanted me to obey Him because He loved that one girl who was just beginning to develop her own fear of God in her life. And He wanted me to come fan that flame and teach her, both in words and actions, what it means to live a life that is built around a deep respect for God. He wanted her to grow to love Him.

Mentoring that one girl eventually led to a small group that grew and continued for thirteen years. That one act of obedience led to my trying to get published. Yes . . . after five years and nineteen rejections, God eventually opened those doors, giving me the opportunity to write three books for teen girls. I've been speaking to young women now for more than fifteen years. I absolutely love it! Give me a room full of authentic, ready-to-grab-life girls and I am ready to invest. Now, I feel confident around them because **confident is what I have become in Him**. Walking out the fear of the Lord and following His calling has developed in me a confidence I could never have discovered otherwise.

This growth that has taken place in my life began with the same seeds that were planted in the lives of Shiphrah and Puah: "The midwives, however, feared God and did not do what the king of Egypt had told them to do; they let the boys live" (Exodus 1:17). The fear of God was in them in the beginning.

They feared God more than they feared a man who had the power to kill them! This reverence, awe, and submission compelled them to do the hard thing. Empowered them to do it scared. It is exactly the same answer Peter and the apostles gave hundreds of years later when they were in a similar, dangerous situation. Pulled before a court and threatened for their act of sharing that Jesus was the Son of God, they replied to the authorities, "We must obey God rather than human beings" (Acts 5:29).

Peter and the apostles were not the only ones whose actions were determined because of their fear of God.

Read Genesis 22, the story of Abraham and his son Isaac. What action did God ask Abraham to take? How did God honor Abraham because Abraham feared him (22:12)?

_____

_____

_____

_____

_____

_____

Were Shiphrah, Puah, Jochebed, Miriam, Peter, and Abraham all afraid in their situations? I'm sure they were. Most likely much more afraid than I was to invite over a group of high schoolers.

Yet, we all had something in common: We had to do it afraid. And you can too. I know we don't *want* to, but when we make the choice that we want to obey God more than we want anything else, that *want* will fuel us with the faith we need to move forward.

Nothing builds our confidence like doing fearsome things *with* God. Doing scary things with God is the action where the seed of confidence is planted into the soil of fearing Him. This is the perfect condition for Christ Confidence to grow. When, in complete trust, we depend on Him, a deep assurance can settle in our soul, even though we are still scared.

Even in chaos, when we know we are right where God wants us, we can experience His confidence.

In Luke 1:50, in what my Bible titles "Mary's Song," what does Jesus' mother say is a benefit to those who fear Him?

_____

_____

_____

_____

_____

_____

But what if you don't already have the fear of God? In the times we are living in now, when so many do not believe in absolute truth, many of us have not been raised to fear God. The good news is you can develop or grow the fear of God in your life.

The fear of God can grow in our lives as we get to know Him. The more we get to know God, digging into His Word to learn more and more about who He is, what His character looks like, how He thinks and acts, the awesomeness of His majesty compels us to fear Him.

This mighty tree of confidence that begins to grow tall can withstand winds and storms because it is a confidence that is deep. It is not standing on ground that moves like the sand when the tide comes in and out. The reason we make the choices we make to do the things we do is because we never want to offend this One who loves us so very much. Instead, we want to return deep love with deep love. And the absolutely beautiful thing is when this fear of God grows, it develops into a passion for Him that can stand firm against anything . . . even the threat of a king.

Apply It

Up to this point in your relationship with God, what have you understood "the fear of the Lord" to mean?

_____

_____

_____

_____

How has that changed after our week of studying together?

_____

_____

_____

_____

Friend, this week you have planted a seed in the good soil of learning to fear the Lord. As we continue to dig into God's Word together, we will learn more about Him, His character, and His heart.

As we finish up, ask the Holy Spirit to develop in you a deep awe and respect for our holy God. Ask Him to reveal to you, in a way you have never experienced before, His deep and boundless love so that your fear of Him will grow more and more.

Group Discussion Questions

Start by reading this week's memory verse aloud as a group, or select an individual to do so:

"For the LORD will be your confidence and will keep your foot from being caught."—Proverbs 3:26 (ESV)

1. Considering Lynn's stories, what are some examples of snares we can get caught in when we lack confidence? What are some examples of your confidence facing adversity?

2. Did you grow up "fearing God" in one way or another? Was it a healthy fear, full of respect and awe, or was it unhealthy, literal fear?

3. Share with the group a time when you were called to account for something and felt you had to make a choice of allegiance or loyalty. Perhaps a time when you had to choose between this world and God's will or command? What did you do? Why?

4. Why is the fear of people such a big barrier to us walking in God's confidence?

5. In our study this week we read 1 Peter 3:15. Read together 1 Peter 3:14. How does the motto "Do It Scared" fit with this verse, and what does it mean in your life today?

6. What do you resonate with most about the example of confidence we have through the Women of Exodus?

Go around the group and share what the fear of God means to you personally today.

End your time together praying for each woman to be full of confidence through her personal fear of God rather than her fear of earthly approval.

The Daughters of 3

WHEN CONFIDENCE IS CHALLENGED

★

PRAYER: *Jesus, I'm so looking forward to learning new things in Your Word. You say in Hebrews 4:12, "For the word of God is alive and active. Sharper than any double-edged sword, it penetrates even to dividing soul and spirit, joints and marrow; it judges the thoughts and attitudes of the heart." This is what I want. I want Your Word to go into my soul and spirit, taking my thoughts and attitudes to where Your life in me gives me Your confidence. Thank you for the gift of Your Word; I am ready for it to do Your work. In Jesus' name, Amen.*

MEMORY VERSE: "But blessed is the one who trusts in the LORD, whose confidence is in him."—Jeremiah 17:7

★

Stuck

I WAS IN WAY OVER MY HEAD . . . and I knew it.

Trying to land my first professional job in a way-too-big city, I had been entirely too ambitious. Having moved five hours from my small-town home, I was in desperate need of a job to fund this big step. If I tanked, what would I do? Certain that I had oversold myself, my mind began to spin.

What have I done? Am I really as competent as I said I was? What about all the jargon I don't know? Why, oh why did I interview for this position? Am I even capable of this? What was I thinking? I don't even have a college degree! I should have just stuck with what I am comfortable with because now I'm really in trouble!

My mind kept pushing me closer and closer to the cliff of failure. I couldn't take the doubt inside of me. Skepticism stole my peace by day and my sleep by night.

I decided I just couldn't sit around and wait for failure. On my first day, I located the Human Resources department, sat down with the gal who hired me and . . . talked myself right out of the job. Yes, I did! My employer was kind enough to find another position for me in another department that didn't require me to dress a certain way or sit at a high-profile desk. My new position (in the warehouse) was out of sight—and probably out of my employers' mind.

How's that for lacking confidence?

Are you that woman? If so, you won't be for long.

Maybe you've talked yourself out of so many opportunities that you question whether or not you *can* actually move forward. In fact, numb could describe how you feel on many days, simply surviving.

Don't be too hard on yourself! Surviving is not actually an entirely bad place to be. We all want more than survival though. We want to know we matter. We want to live a life that makes a difference and in that process experience joy, peace, and hope—the abundant life Jesus spoke of.

I've discovered that finding confidence often means making a move when (and most often when) I think I can't!

Remember that skydiving jump? Honestly, I didn't think I had it in me.

Sometimes we have to do what we need to do even when we don't have the confidence to do it. And the process of doing the thing we need to do when we don't have the confidence to do it is just what helps us *find* the confidence we need!

Sometimes we have to do what we need to do without the confidence to do it.

I think God actually orchestrates this whole thing, putting us in situations that demand our dependence on Him. That's how it appears to me as I've been studying the Bible.

So . . . good news, then! You're in great company. If you feel like your confidence is lacking or lost, then it's the perfect time to act. *Make your move especially when you think you can't!*

To make this move, we're going to need at least enough confidence to get us moving a bit. So, let's start by defining what confidence means.

According to dictionary.com, confidence means: "full trust; belief in the powers, trustworthiness, or reliability of a person or thing."[8]

I have confidence that my car will start when I insert the key. I have confidence that my house will cool off when I turn on my air conditioner and that my coffee will make me feel cozy in the winter.

But what about when the thing we place our trust in doesn't come through?

There was a group of women in the Bible who experienced just that. What they were counting on didn't come through. It forced them into a precarious situation—not by choice but by default.

To give us a bit of context, we'll go back to Exodus 2 again, when God's people were slaves in Egypt. They cried out to God to set them free. God heard their cries and called a man named Moses to lead them out of Egypt and move them to a new home: the Promised Land.

The next book in the Bible, Numbers, is the setting for our story. The word *Numbers* is a Hebrew title meaning "in the wilderness" as it tells of the trip from Egypt, through the wilderness, to the Promised Land. A two-hundred-mile journey, that should have lasted approximately two weeks, took the Israelites over forty years. The Israelites wandered in this wide and vast desert space, often as a result of their own choices, which led to a disconnect with God.

We're going to enter this narrative at a very exciting time. Toward the end of this journey, God calls for a census to be taken before the Israelites can finally leave the wilderness and move into the Promised Land.

God qualifies exactly who is to be counted in Numbers 26:4: "men twenty years old or more." It is important to note not just the age but also the sex God calls to be counted in the census. (You can read the entire inventory of names in Numbers 26.) In verse 33, we meet for the first time the women we are going to zero in on and the *only* women listed in the entire 65-verse genealogy (except for a daughter of Asher):

> "(Zelophehad son of Hepher had no sons; he had only daughters, whose names were Mahlah, Noah, Hoglah, Milkah and Tirzah.)"

Whether I call them the daughters of Zelophehad or Mahlah, Noah, Hoglah, Milkah, and Tirzah, their names are as long to type as they are hard to pronounce! For the sake of time and writer's cramp, let's call them the daughters of Z.

Zelophehad is singled out for one reason: He had no sons.

God then describes to Moses how the land was to be divided among the tribes, specifically to the sons of each tribe.

This reminds me of my extended family. Both of my parents came from farming families in Minnesota. While my parents stopped farming before I was born, many of their siblings continued. As my uncles began aging, they started passing on the family farms to my cousins, keeping the land, and the inheritance, in the family. As I think about my extended family, I can't think of any of my relatives who are passing on their farm to their daughters. Each of my uncles is passing on his farm to one or more of his sons.

This is similar to what is happening in Numbers 26. The land is being divided up among the sons of the tribes of Israel.

This situation is where we find our potentially-out-of-confidence women.

Digging Deeper

Read Numbers 27:1–4.

Numbers 26:33 tells us Zelophehad had no sons, but it is not until chapter 27 that we discover Zelophehad is dead. Not only has he passed away, but Numbers 27 also makes it clear that his daughters were without brothers, husbands, or sons.

Single women with no father, no brothers, no husband, and no sons in this culture meant *no land*. Because of the tradition of handing down property only to men, these women were not going to get *any* acreage as the Promise Land was divided.

So where are they supposed to live? How would they take care of themselves?

Women have come a long way since ancient Bible times. While some women without means can still face similar problems, most women today are able to find work, get a paycheck, and find a place to live. Imagine how much different our lives would be if this were 1800s America instead of 2000s America. *None of us*, simply because we are women, would be permitted to own land. Without the chance for landownership, all of us would be completely dependent on a man (father, husband, or son) to provide housing of some sort. Where would we live if we didn't have a man?

That is what the daughters of Z were facing: homelessness.

They were stuck.

Describe a time in your life when you have felt stuck. A time when a solution to a problem seemed like it just couldn't be found.

_____

_____

_____

_____

_____

The culture these women lived in presented only one way for their provision: a man. And they didn't have a single one! It would appear that they had no choice, but in fact they did. They had the choice to accept the voices of their culture as well as the whispers in their own heads, or they could make their move.

Make the move they needed to make even if they didn't have the confidence to make it.

Reread Numbers 27:2–4.

What advance did these ladies make?

_____

_____

Why was this a big deal?

_____

_____

Describe a time in your life when you were low on confidence, but had a big need for it.

_____

_____

Read Exodus 25:1–9.

Numbers 27:2 tells us that the daughters approached "the entrance to the tent of meeting." Based on Exodus 25:8, what is the significance of this place where the daughters met with the Israelite leadership?

_____

_____

This was the time before God's people "were filled with the Holy Spirit" (Acts 2:4). Where God's Spirit dwelt was crucial to how the people related to Him. The Tent of Meeting was where the priests and Moses went to meet and consult with God. So, when the daughters of Z approached the Tent of Meeting to speak with Moses, they were going to meet with the one God had appointed to be their intermediary.

It could be compared to our modern-day going to court.

There the gals are, in a state of despair, looking for justice.

Read Psalm 82:3–4. What do these verses tell us about God's view on the most vulnerable of society?

_____

_____

The women knew God's heart toward the weak, fatherless, poor, oppressed, and needy. They knew because that is exactly who the Israelites were when they were slaves in Egypt. And what had God done? He had brought them justice and rescued them from Pharaoh. _This_ was the God whom the women served. He defended the Israelites cause before the Egyptians, and He would defend the cause of these homeless women now.

Yet even knowing that, the women would be required to step out. They believed God said the land was for _every one_ of His people, and that included them. Still, they would have to be vulnerable. Their actions show that they trusted that God would reward their vulnerability; He would care for them.

Maybe today you are feeling just as vulnerable as the daughters of Z might have felt. You sense God nudging you. Maybe you have felt compelled to a specific action, but instead of finding the land of opportunity, you've reached a dead end. No right, no left, no options, and you don't have what you need or what it takes to create any.

Stuck!

That's where the daughters of Z were too.

Yet, the sisters decided they wouldn't give up even though it seemed everything was against them. Stuck and stopped are not the same thing! They believed what the Lord said was true. They chose to move.

> _Stuck and stopped_
> _are not the same thing._

Look at these gals!

They didn't shrink back because that is "just the way it was" or hide behind their culture's norms. Their society said "normal" was having a man provide a place for them to live. They did not let that message paralyze them from finding a solution to their problem. They refused to remain stuck.

We don't have the chance to get inside the heads of the daughters of Z, but I can only imagine doubt and fear might have come rolling in before they made their move. *No one has ever done this before. Who do we think we are? What will the leaders think of us? Will the women of our community think we're too bold? Troublemakers? What if the panel of men say no?*

Our fear of failure can push us down before we even get up. The majority of our battle with confidence happens in our head. We listen to what has been said and what we have told ourselves and we believe it. This is why God makes it so clear that we need to write His Word on our hearts (Proverbs 7:3).

I'd love to think that I am as bold and sure of God's promises as the daughters of Z, but that's not always so. Culture constantly makes us aware of "our place" and challenges whether we have what it takes. *Who do you think you are?* For me, my lack of education has been a source of insecurity. *Who am I to share with you what I've learned in God's Word?* Maybe you hear these deafening whispers too.

In life, there will be times when we have to do what we need to do even when we don't have the confidence to do it. This is the perfect setup for God to show up. Stuck and stopped are not the same to Him. He can and will help us make our move. He has promised us, "[We] can do all this through him who gives [us] strength" (Philippians 4:13). I am going to take Him up on it! Won't you too?

Apply It

I look at the daughters and wonder *why* and *how* they acted so boldly. How did they go against the norms of their culture to get what they believed God had for them? No one, especially the leaders of their tribe, would have expected the women to ask for land because no one had ever done that before. Their faith was groundbreaking.

Tomorrow, we will begin our search to understand why the daughters of Z had the level of confidence they had in a situation where their confidence made no sense.

For today, begin by simply sharing with God where you might be feeling stuck. Ask Him, like the daughters of Z, what is the move He would have you take in His strength.

DAY TWO

★

Build One Another Up

MEMORY VERSE: "But blessed is the one who trusts in the Lord, whose confidence is in him."—Jeremiah 17:7

WOW COULD SHE SING! As I watched my TV screen, a young girl, maybe ten or eleven years of age, belted out the national anthem like I had never heard before. Her darkened glasses, though inside an arena, revealed she was visually impaired. Yet neither her age nor her disability held her back from sharing her gift with all those who were blessed to hear her.

Where did she get confidence like that? Did it have something to do with her parents? What had her teachers said to help her become so brave? Was there a doctor in her life pushing her forward?

These are the types of questions I often find myself asking, so it wasn't uncommon that I found myself wondering the same things about the daughters of Z. What was the source of their confidence? We're not specifically told in the Scripture of anyone speaking confidence into their lives.

I am blessed to have many encouraging people pouring into my life. My husband constantly encourages me. Friends tell me to keep going even with my latest rejections, and my kids often encourage me with their texts. How did the daughters of Z, who apparently had no one, gain the confidence they needed to go before such powerful men in their community, including Moses himself? Weren't they intimidated?

Digging Deeper

Looking at clues provided in Scripture, let's start with what we *don't* know about these women:

1. Their ages

There isn't one word about the ages of these five daughters. We know from Numbers 36 they were single, and in Jewish tradition, girls married young—twelve to fourteen years old. Maybe they were *really* young, or maybe they were older and had just never married.

We just don't know.

Like the daughters of Z, I am one of five daughters. In fact, I am the youngest of five daughters; number seven of eight kids. It can be a bit of a struggle to find your place when you're in a big family, let alone one of the youngest. Although we might make an issue of age, we know God doesn't. When it comes to being used by God, age does not matter.

Read 1 Timothy 4:12.

What does Paul tell his mentee, Timothy, in regard to how he should allow others to treat him because of his youth?

_____

_____

Does your community encourage young people to use their gifts and talents, or do the older members fill most of the needs?

_____

_____

The daughters of Z could have been teen girls when this situation took place, and if they were, their youth did not matter to God.

Conversely, they could have been older women—and it still wouldn't have mattered.

Read Job 12:12.

How does or does not our culture emulate this verse?

_____

_____

_____

If the daughters of Z were older, according to Job 12:12, age was on their side!

2. Their appearance

Again, we know nothing. Nada. Zilch. Zero. Not a single word is said, *nothing at all*, about their appearance. Tall, small, heavy, thin, dark skin or lighter?

Since the Bible doesn't tell us anything about their appearance, I'm drawing this conclusion: These details didn't matter in the daughters of Z's story because appearance doesn't matter. Appearance does not affect God's will for them or us.

We put people in categories based on what we see. *We* decide just how far someone can go. *We* decide if we think they are the wrong size, wrong sex, or wrong shade. **God never does**. He never has and never will.

> *Neither our contour nor our color affect God's calling.*

Read 1 Samuel 16:7.

In our culture, community, and churches, in what way do we make it clear appearance *does* matter to us?

_____

_____

Culture tries its hardest to make the external all too important. It's hard not to do the same and judge each other even within the body of Christ. Ladies, no one is worse at this than us!

Like smoke from burning pancakes, the tension in the stifling air rose. We waited shoulder-to-shoulder for the doors to open. The concert promised to be the best of the year, but the frustration with the stuffy space was sucking all the happiness out of me. My husband and I tried to make the best of the situation, making small talk about our day, when suddenly, a grimace of sorts came across his face. The question followed: "Why, when a woman walks in the room, do all the other women size her up?"

Oh no! He noticed! He knows!

Honestly, I wanted to lie to cover for us. I thought this thing we women do was known only to us and totally on the inside. I had no idea guys could see or sense the unspoken judgment we pass on each other. How do I explain to a guy the deep insecurity we girls all too often struggle with? Even as I began, I could just hear how sad the truth sounded.

This notion we have, that *her* beauty, *her* success and *her* confidence detracts from me and mine, slowly seeps into our hearts undetected. Infiltrating our hearts and minds, it's a deception that poisons the way we think of our teammates, our *sisters*! It demands control over how we think, speak, and act toward one another.

Even if we make up our minds to fight it, like a terrible infection, it returns unwanted again and again. It's a lie and a powerful one at that.

Pulling us in, this horrible wrong sucks us under—before we've even spoken a word.

What's worse is that we can even feel like we're not to blame—our upbringing or society is. Regardless, we need to call *it* what *it* is: sin. Judgment is sin.

Paul shares the cure for our illness, and I don't know about you, but it's a tough pill for me to swallow.

Read Romans 13:8–10.

How do you think this Scripture applies when it comes to the way we women judge one another's appearance?

_____

_____

_____

_____

Maybe you've heard, as I have, that Jesus paid it all. That in Him we have no debt. And it's true that when we ask, He forgives us for all of our sins just as 1 John 1:9 tells us. This passage in Romans 13 makes it clear, though: We *do* have a debt. We have an obligation to love one another, and that means breaking the girl code. When it comes to cutting another down, we have a command to do the complete opposite: Build her up. First Thessalonians 5:11 tells us, "Therefore encourage one another and build each other up." Love does no harm to a neighbor, not ever.

> *When it comes to cutting a sister down,*
> *God commands us to build her up.*

God doesn't qualify or disqualify anyone based on our looks. How could He? He created us! Friends, it's time we stop disqualifying each other and ourselves.

Here's what we *do* know about the daughters of Z:

► They were single. Numbers 36 makes this fact clear.

► They were from a large family.

► The daughters didn't fit in. They had no father, brothers, husbands, or sons to provide for them in a society where men were required for survival.

► We also know their heritage.

When I was growing up, I liked to make up stories of relatives I had that were brave, wealthy, and stood up to tradition. Key word: *made-up*.

Every Monday and Wednesday of third grade, the big, yellow paneled truck would pull into the parking-lot-turned-playground-at-noon at St. Patrick's Catholic School. *Martin Brothers*, painted in big, bold, black letters on the side revealed the owners' names. I decided it was a good idea to tell my friends this business belonged to my dad and his brother. (Insecurity can be really powerful, even in third grade!) They did not own that business. My dad worked in the brass foundry down the street; his brother worked at a school. But the power of that story, even in my case a story that wasn't even true, made me feel confident. It made me feel like I was a somebody.

Stories can have so much power in our lives; especially stories of our heritage. They can define us and have the ability to pull us up or put us down.

I can't help but think that the same thing happened in the lives of the daughters of Zelophehad. They had a very confident grandfather that they may have gained confidence from as well. We'll learn more about him in our next section.

We need to remember that love never does harm to a neighbor. Because we are loved, we can confidently choose to love others, never cutting down and only building up our sisters in Christ.

Apply It

How has your age and appearance influenced your confidence level?

_____

_____

How has age and appearance impacted how you view others?

_____

_____

Many influences that come in and out of our lives have the power to impact how we view others. Some common prejudices include: age, ability, class, color, sex/gender, weight, economic status, and country of origin. Take a few moments with the Lord. Go over this list, one by one, and ask Him to reveal to you two things:

1. How do you hold a prejudice against others in each of these areas?
2. How do you feel prejudice, in any of the categories, has impacted your life?

Where you have discriminated against others, ask Jesus to forgive you. Ask Him to begin to open your eyes to see how prejudicial thinking is affecting your day-to-day life. Pray for power to overcome these negative thoughts toward others so that you can be a force of change in this world through His love.

Ask Him to show you where you need healing from experiencing prejudice. Pray for the power to forgive those who have held you back and changed the way you see and feel about yourself through their words and actions.

★

It's All in the Family

MEMORY VERSE: "But blessed is the one who trusts in the LORD, whose confidence is in him."—Jeremiah 17:7

WHAT A DISCOVERY! When my mother revealed to me in elementary school that I was related to the American President James Garfield, I took full advantage of the confidence this gave me. Being related to someone famous—didn't that make me important? (I've since learned my great, great, great grandpa and President Garfield's father were second cousins. So glad I didn't know back then just how far apart the connection actually was!)

The daughters of Zelophehad had much more to be proud of than I!

Numbers 27:1 reveals the famous patriarch Joseph was actually in their direct ancestral line; he was the sisters' great-great-great-great grandfather.

In what way might it have mattered that the daughters of Z were related to Joseph?

_____

_____

_____

In Jewish culture, passing on family stories was very important, even commanded by God in Deuteronomy 4:9: "Only be careful, and watch yourselves closely so that you do not forget the things your eyes have seen or let them fade from your heart as long as you live. Teach them to your children and to their children after them."

Similar commands to teach our children our histories with God can be found in Deuteronomy 6:7 and Deuteronomy 11:19. At times in Israel's history, God even tells them to write a song to be taught to the Israelites so they would sing it and not forget His words (Deuteronomy 31:19–22; 32:1–43).

Based on these verses, I have no doubt these gals would have grown up hearing about their great-great-great-great grandfather, Joseph. Joseph represented the epitome of the word *confidence*.

Digging Deeper

<u>Read Joseph's story beginning in Genesis 37:1–4.</u>

Why was Joseph "Daddy's favorite"?

_____

_____

<u>Read Genesis 37:5–11.</u>

Have you ever had any dreams that you believed were from God?

_____

_____

Joseph's life would have many twists and turns as well as many, many years before these spiritually-significant dreams would come to pass.

<u>Read Genesis 37:12–36.</u>

List a few of the things Joseph lost or had taken from him.

_____

_____

_____

_____

_____

Here are a few I found:

▷ Joseph's brothers sold him into slavery. He lost his family.

▷ Joseph became a slave. He lost his freedom.

▷ Joseph lived in a foreign country. He lost his home.

▷ If you choose to read on in Genesis 39 and 40, you'll see that when convicted of a crime he didn't commit, Joseph lost his reputation and his position. Thrown into prison and forgotten, he lost his future (or so it would appear).

What was the *one thing*, through it all, that Joseph didn't lose?
His confidence in God's promises.

His confidence was the one thing he didn't lose or have taken from him. Though all else was taken, his confidence in God and in the future he believed God had for him was never lost.

God Himself was the one thing Joseph had even when all else was gone.

And because of Joseph's confidence in his Father God, Joseph never quit believing. He never gave up.

Let's begin looking at a few things we can discover about Joseph that might tell us *why* he was so confident.

Read Genesis 39 and 41.

List a few ways Joseph demonstrated confidence in these chapters.

_____

_____

_____

_____

Remembering what we read in Genesis 37 and using the new information we just gained in Genesis 39 and 41, here are a few facts that stand out from Joseph's life:

1. Like the daughters of Z, Joseph was also single.

2. He, too, came from a large family, a *very* large family. He was one of twelve sons.

3. He didn't fit in the culture where he was living as a slave.

4. According to Genesis 39:6b, he "was well-built and handsome." Appearance here *does* matter because it becomes a detail of his story. It gets Joseph in trouble since his boss's wife makes a move on him, calls it rape when he resists, and Joseph is thrown in prison.

We also know, based on his actions, Joseph had a confidence that stuck.

I can't help but think that just as I found confidence in the stories of my relatives, both real and not so real, the daughters of Zelophehad built theirs on the very real story of Joseph. Growing up hearing of Joseph's brave confidence may have empowered them too!

➤ He wasn't afraid to stand up to Potiphar's wife when she made a move on him (Genesis 39).

➤ He wasn't too intimidated to interpret Pharaoh's dream (Genesis 41:1–39).

▶ He showed no fear when he was made second in charge to Pharaoh of all of Egypt—at the age of thirty (Genesis 41:41–57). I didn't have confidence that looked anything like that at thirty!

Culture commands us to build our confidence on things that God does not, such as age and appearance. Joseph's life is a demonstration that confidence built on God can withstand even the most confidence-defeating situations.

Apply It

In both the lives of Joseph and the daughters of Z, family actions and stories had a monumental impact on their lives. They can on our own lives as well. We can believe things about ourselves that can empower us or imprison us.

When we look at our own family histories, we, too, have stories we have heard or witnessed that have impacted our own level of confidence.

Briefly describe one positive story (like the daughters of Z) that you can lean into and/or one negative story (like Joseph's) that you need to put behind you. Then, finish your time today by thanking the Lord for those positive influences and asking Him to do His deep work to heal you of those that were negative.

_____

_____

_____

_____

_____

_____

★

Some Place and Some One Are Shaky Ground

MEMORY VERSE: "But blessed is the one who trusts in the LORD, whose confidence is in him."—Jeremiah 17:7

BEFORE I WAS BORN, my parents took many courageous steps to try to better their lives. These brave actions meant that my life would look significantly different than each of their childhoods.

Moving from the state they had grown up in, they took their family and started a new life in a new state. They left behind generations of farming to seek out more security. They stepped out of what was comfortable to discover and encounter God in a personal way. They left the formal worship their families had practiced for generations to find a new intimacy with God.

Their bravery became my example of not looking to the temporary things of life for security. Believing God was directing me too, six weeks before school began, I withdrew my college enrollment. Instead, I chose to move over a thousand miles from home to attend a training school for those who felt called to ministry. Preparing to leave behind a boyfriend I planned to marry when I returned, I packed my things to go to a place I had never seen. My parents drove me to the training school on a ranch in the middle of a Texas range. Within an hour, they were back on the long road home. I was left in what felt like a foreign land where I knew no one. The terrain was different and the people spoke with a different accent. Believing God had told me to go, I unpacked my things and with timidity, prepared for what God had for me next.

Like my parents before me, I bravely did what I felt I was called to do, not what felt comfortable. They had taught me, through their actions, confidence doesn't come from a place.

As I had learned from my parents, maybe the daughters of Z learned from Joseph not to build your confidence on a place. Joseph lost his place, his father's wealthy estate, when his brothers sold him. In the foreign land of Egypt, no one would have cared about his rich father's business far, far away. If Joseph had built his confidence on a place, his confidence would have disappeared just like he did from the pasture.

For many reasons, places are important to us. We find comfort in the stability of our homes and dream of owning one of our own one day. We have been taught that the fulfillment of that dream is a mile-marker of success and stability. Working hard, we sacrifice, sometimes the things we shouldn't—time with our family and being generous—in order to achieve this pinnacle: a place of our own.

Through the life of Joseph and through stories of our own friends and family, we know that this sometimes-illusive idea of obtaining a "home" is a dangerous place to put our trust. All too often, things outside of our control strip us of our places . . . and take our confidence with it. The daughters of Z didn't have a "place" on which to build their trust. They had no home and yet here, in their homelessness, they demonstrated you don't need a place of your own to have the confidence of God. We don't need a someplace in order to put our trust in Him.

The daughters of Z, hearing their grandfather's story, could have learned that Joseph didn't base his confidence on some*one*, certainly not his family. Genesis 37:4 says, "[His brothers] hated him and could not speak a kind word to him." If anything, his family's rejection would have caused him to *lose* whatever self-esteem he had. He couldn't have found confidence in his marriage or children because he wasn't married and didn't have children when he experienced all his trouble. Joseph didn't build his confidence on some*one* because he didn't have a some*one*.

After finishing the training school program, my life came to an intersection. I had to decide what to do next. A thousand miles from home, I needed a plan . . . and the confidence to move, not back home, but almost four thousand miles away to continue my schooling. Because I was still young, and my original plan had been to go back home and marry my boyfriend, I contacted my parents, seeking affirmation for my next steps.

Affirmation is not really what you would call my father's words. In fact, he said he didn't want me moving so far away until *after* I was married.

After I was married? Honestly, his words really irritated me. *Why* after *I'm married?* My boyfriend and I had broken up and there wasn't anyone waiting in the wings! This was all I could think as my dad shared his thoughts. Though I didn't agree, I respected his advice. I believed God was using him to speak to me (even though it didn't feel like it made sense).

I wonder if Joseph ever experienced pressure to find a spouse and begin a family, which I often see in the lives of the singles I love. It's as if there is some sort of time clock, ticking away, sending the covert message: *Your life doesn't begin until you're someone's someone.*

Sometimes, like my father said to me, we can say to our Father God, "I can't move forward until my relationship status changes."

Read 1 Corinthians 7:8, 34–35.

Paul's advice goes directly against my dad's, I know!

How do you see Paul's wisdom played out in your own life if you are single or in the life of one you know who is single?

Paul goes on to shoot straight with the Corinthians: "But those who marry will face many troubles in this life, and I want to spare you this" (1 Corinthians 7:28).

Paul states that the greatest status *is* single status. If you are single and are able to see this and direct your energies to serving your First Love, Paul says you have the opportunity to reach your potential distraction-free! Key word: *if.*

Here is another opportunity to go against culture's message that you need someone to be someone, to not base our "success" on whether or not we have a significant other. Yes, God absolutely created relationships. He created Adam . . . and then He created Eve. Rich and intimate relationships enhance our lives, making them richer and fuller. But we do not need *someone* to complete us. We are not "less than" or a partial person until we find someone. We are already complete in Christ; deeply loved by Him.

It is on this truth that we build our self-worth: we are the bride of Christ. *This* relationship status will last forever and will forever stay the same!

Our reality is that any one of us could go to bed married tonight and find ourselves alone tomorrow, while the reverse could also be true. Not so in our relationship with the Lord! Song of Songs 6:3 tells us, "I am my beloved's and my beloved is mine." And that is not going to change!

Wise Joseph didn't build his confidence on the faulty foundation of a human relationship status.

Although I didn't completely grasp the whats and whys of her actions, as a young girl I witnessed my mother reading her Bible every day. Sitting in her chair with God's Word in her lap, she began each day by filling her heart with God's truth.

Growing up, Mom's family life was more than shaky. She had not seen unconditional love; quite the opposite. At the time when she came to know Jesus in a personal way, her confidence was all but gone. She had come to know Him out of her desperation. As she built her newfound faith, she began to overcome her unstable confidence, and by doing so she taught me how powerful our God is. I learned by watching her: True security comes from Someone, Jesus.

When we truly understand who we are and Whose we are, our lives are radically changed!

> *When we truly understand who we are and Whose we are, our lives are radically changed!*

Emerging from the van, the stench pushed me back. Having never witnessed deep poverty like this before, the raw sewage and animal waste filling the trench-lined streets caught me off guard. Even the fumes couldn't extinguish my excitement for the day, though. This day, my friend Amy Carroll and I were witnessing firsthand the life change God was bringing to small, slum communities through the work of Mission India.

Steps from our vehicle, Josh, our Mission India host, led us to the home we were invited to visit.

Slipping off my shoes, I stepped across the threshold and there she stood. Strong. Beaming.

The soft, delicate, blush-shaded sari swirled around her slender frame as Sunita stood at the entrance greeting us. Her gentle, yet sparkling eyes twinkled as a smile swept her sun-worn face.

Her grace in this residence of deprivation, her loveliness amidst the stench of sewage and sights of scarcity, were so out of place.

Josh introduced this woman, now recognized in her community as a leader, as a woman who brings change. She had not always been.

Unable to read or perform basic math, Sunita had been trapped in poverty without these necessary life skills. Sunita is a part of a social class that for centuries told those in it that they are worth less than nothing.

This social class is not small. Hundreds of millions of Indians have been trapped in poverty, and continue to be, simply because of the origin of their birth.

Her culture has also told her of another strike against her: She is a woman. She has been told from her very beginning that she has no value; she is an untouchable.

Then several years ago, Sunita was invited to a literacy class by Mission India, where she would be given the one thing she had never experienced: opportunity. She took it.

In this Bible-based class, Sunita gained not only the power to read and calculate, but she met Jesus. Her life was transformed. Her religion had taught her, based on the social class of her birth, she was less than nothing. The cows roaming the streets of this village were of greater worth than Sunita.

Through the Mission India literacy class, the lies spoken over her and to her were slowly stripped away. Sunita began to see just how the One True God saw her, as His precious daughter, His bride, the one He was compelled by love to come for. Through the Scripture shared in the literacy books, she learned that she was not worth less than nothing; just as Proverbs 31:10 says, she was worth more than rubies!

This was what I saw beaming through Sunita's smile and the joy radiating from her eyes. Eyes that before would have only looked at the ground now could look me eye-to-eye. She is of great worth and now she knows.

Through our translator, we began to hear her story. With this new and powerful knowledge of Christ, Sunita's heart began to burn to bring this life-changing Truth to the women of her community. She became an informal teacher, bringing her newfound hope to the poor in her slum. When five families in community came to know Christ, she was inspired to become a project manager, overseeing five Mission India literacy classes.

The confidence Sunita found in Christ was contagious. Sitting in the classroom that afternoon, I could see the same sparkle I witnessed in her eyes on the faces of the beautiful Indian students in that room. They had gained knowledge; they could read to their children and calculate their costs at the market. But they were obtaining so very much more: confidence in their newfound identity as the bride of Christ.

What changed Sunita was truth. Truth changed the way she thought about herself, and when her thinking changed, she changed.

Like Sunita, we can gain God's confidence when we fill our hearts and minds with His truth. When we build our confidence on Someone: Jesus.

Apply It

As you reflect on your life, where can you see in your past or in your present that you have built your confidence on someplace or on someone?

_____

_____

Today, write out this week's memory verse on your phone notes or a small card that can fit in your pocket. Set an alarm to remind yourself midway through your day to reflect on this truth: "But blessed is the one who trusts in the LORD, whose confidence is in him" (Jeremiah 17:7).

_____

_____

_____

★

Some Thing Has Got to Go

MEMORY VERSE: "But blessed is the one who trusts in the LORD, whose confidence is in him."—Jeremiah 17:7

YESTERDAY WE REFLECTED ON JOSEPH and the foundation of his confidence. We saw that clearly he did not build his confidence on someplace or someone. He lacked both of these and yet demonstrated an unshakable faith in His God.

Joseph's story also reveals that he didn't build his confidence on something. If Joseph had built his confidence on something, such as his family's wealth, it would have slipped away the moment his new owner started the long trip to Egypt. Yet it never did.

The things we own can give us so much happiness and just as quickly cause us so much sorrow. So shiny and new, they glitter and twinkle as they promise boundless bliss. We work hard, sacrifice our time, energy, sometimes even our emotions to obtain them. Our hearts tell us, "When I finally get ＿＿＿＿ , then I'll have arrived." Finally, we can be happy and secure.

I know, we've been told: "Follow your heart." But that has been very unwise advice. In fact, God's Word tells us just the opposite: "The heart is deceitful above all things, and desperately sick; who can understand it?" (Jeremiah 17:9 ESV). We can't follow our hearts. They lie to us! Burdening us, causing us to feel as though we don't have what we "need," we fix our happiness on obtaining what seems out of reach. I know; I've done it and regretted the results.

I've found that all too often these belongings, these things that we had to have, become baggage at some point down the road. The house has to be kept up, taking away time from those I love. Other possessions come first with payments, later with repairs. The resources I would have shared with others instead are used to keep my "thing" going. When times are hard and the thing we *had* to have, now needs to go, will our confidence go with it?

There are so many "things" that can fill the description of *our* something: decorating, fashion, makeup, fitness, vacations, nature, career, and the list goes on. They have all been my "thing" at some stage of my life. They are not bad; in fact, most of them are good. But things are to be the "add-ons" in life, the icing on the cake, not the substance of it. When we look to things to fill the deep needs of our hearts, we are regularly disappointed.

Take a moment to reflect on your life. List some things you have used to bring you happiness and security.

_____

_____

_____

_____

What has been the result?

_____

_____

_____

_____

<u>Read 1 Corinthians 7:31.</u>

What does Paul warn us about our things?

_____

_____

_____

Sometimes our things are not tangible. Consider knowledge, for instance. _Education? How could gaining more education ever be wrong?_ When we choose to build our confidence on it. When our worth and self-esteem rest on our scholarship, we can slip all too easily into self-reliance and self-righteousness. Anything on which we can build our confidence rather than Christ has the ability to work against us.

Joseph could have easily relied upon his intelligence. He was obviously one smart man to land a job as second in command of all of Egypt! Yet, as we see him interact down the road with his brothers, he lays down his social status that has come with his intellect and success and relates humbly with his brothers (Genesis 42). In fact, like the women of Exodus, he states that the reason for his actions is his fear of God (42:18).

<u>Read 1 Corinthians 1:19–21, 26–31.</u>

Why would God make such a promise in verse 19?

_____

_____

_____

Knowledge is so enticing. Education is good, but there is a line in gaining knowledge where temptation crosses over and we become prideful. We can ask ourselves: For what purpose am I learning? To build my own self-worth or for the purpose of glorifying God? If we look at Genesis 3:6, we can read how giving honor to God was not Eve's motivation for gaining knowledge because she disobeyed God in order to obtain it. Life is dangerous when our confidence is based on our knowledge. There will always be someone smarter or wiser to knock us off the top.

What if Joseph's something that he built his confidence on was his looks? We're told he was handsome. This ended up being the very thing that got Joseph thrown in prison; his asset caused him a deficit! He lost his freedom.

Getting ready for work, the radio commercial arrested me. *Be ideal! Everyone deserves to be their best!* From there, the ad promised to help me get rid of anything I didn't like about my body and replace it with whatever I wanted. As I looked in the mirror, frustration took me over. *Be ideal?* God has already said I *am* ideal! In fact, Song of Songs 4:7 says, "You are altogether beautiful, my darling; there is no flaw in you." That's one to write on your mirror!

Joseph didn't build his confidence on someone, someplace, or something—all things that could and were taken from him. He built his confidence on the one thing *that could not be taken from him*; he built his confidence on God.·

If the daughters of Z had based their confidence on someone, like the men in their family supporting them, they would have had none. Often, we rely on the support or approval of someone to take courageous steps. I don't see that type of support surrounding the sisters, yet they moved forward.

If they had looked to the Israelite leadership remembering them and coming through for them, their confidence would have been gone when they were forgotten. Maybe like me, you've had others say, "We're behind you. Go for it!" Yet, when the time came for action, the backing that was promised was nowhere to be found. The Israelite leadership didn't come *to* the women and say, "It's time you get what you have been waiting for!" The sisters had to push past rejection again and again, persevere, and remind the leadership of what God had promised them. They had to keep their eyes on the One who made the promise.

Having a someone, whether that is a significant other, a best friend, or a supportive family, is wonderful and good for us. Placing all of our faith in them is not.

If the women had based their confidence on someplace, such as having a home, a place where they belonged, their confidence would have faltered. They didn't fit into the standard for their society. They didn't belong. They had to keep their focus on the One to whom they belonged.

If they had based their confidence on something, such as success, education, position, or even physical beauty, as time waned their confidence could have waned as well. They had to keep their confidence on one thing: God's Word. He had said that *all* were to receive an inheritance.

Based on their perseverance, we can determine that the daughters of Z had a confidence that did not come from someone, someplace, or something, but on God, the One who would not forget them. The One who would never change His mind. The One who would keep His promise.

We must not build our confidence on someone, someplace, or something, but on God, the only One that cannot be taken from us.

Apply It

As we wrap up our time this week with the daughters of Z, what have you faced or what are you facing that is blocking the way of you being a more confident you? What is standing in the way of you making your move?

Is it a dream like Joseph's that hasn't come to pass yet, so you've thought: *I guess that wasn't God. Life is passing me by; it's too late now.*

Maybe like the daughters of Z, you have had something taken from you; something has been lost. Your family, your home, your health, your reputation, your hope, or what you thought was your future is gone.

Maybe you've felt that in order to be confident, you needed more. You see others experience the success you want, but you don't have the confidence it takes to step out and take a risk. You've seen others receive the affirmation or the "yes" that you are looking for, and each day you compare yourself to *them*. You know who they are. *No wonder she's confident. I would be too, if I had what she's got. If I just had more.* You think what you don't have is holding you back: a lack of education, opportunity, connections.

I get that. I've been there . . . as in last week. Rejection still comes even after you've experienced success a time or two. I, too, have faced situations when I felt I needed more. I needed more education, more connections, more creativity, more opportunities, more favor, more energy, more personality.

Ask the Holy Spirit to reveal to you what is truly in the way of you stepping out. If specific words come to mind, write them below.

_____

_____

_____

_____

_____

Now, pray and ask Him to do what only He can do.

> *Dear Lord,*
> *I need healing; heal me.*
> *I need to forgive; empower me.*
> *I need courage; fill me.*
> *I need approval; reveal Your approval to me.*
> *I need hope; open my eyes to Yours.*
> *Lord, do in me what only You can do. In Jesus' name, Amen.*

Group Discussion Questions

Read this week's memory verse aloud as a group, or select an individual to do so: "But blessed is the one who trusts in the LORD, whose confidence is in him."—Jeremiah 17:7

1. Consider this statement: "Each time you have attempted to step out in a direction you feel God calling you to, your confidence was challenged." Have you experienced this in your life? Why would this be?

2. What does "stuck and stopped are not the same thing" mean to you today?

3. What do you think is the root of the belief that we don't "deserve" the blessings of God in our lives?

4. Genesis 16:13 says that one of God's names is "the God who sees." When you hear this name, what is the first thought that comes to mind? Share a time in your life when you have felt God *didn't* see you.

5. What do you resonate with most about the example of confidence we have in the daughters of Zelophehad?

Read together Numbers 27:1–2.

It didn't just take courage to approach the Tent of Meeting; these women believed in the Lord, that He is faithful and that He would provide.

End your time together praying one at a time for the confidence of the daughters of Z to approach the Lord and ask for what you need today.

Rahab

WHEN CONFIDENCE IN GOD IS ELUSIVE

★

PRAYER: *Lord, like Rahab, I've made some moves in the past that the world says should define me. You call me to overcome that obstacle to become a confident woman who is defined by faith. Teach me in the days to come that in You I can recover from my defeating past decisions. In You I will make my move toward a strong self-worth, not only changing my life but the lives of those in the future. In Jesus' name, Amen.*

MEMORY VERSE: "Now faith is confidence in what we hope for and assurance about what we do not see." —Hebrews 11:1

★

Hi, My Name Is . . .

I AM SO EXCITED about all we can learn from Rahab, the brave woman of Jericho, found in the book of Joshua. We were introduced to Joshua when he became the Israelites' second leader after Moses's death. Rahab's story takes place right in the middle of the story of the daughters of Zelophehad, after they had approached Moses for their land but before they had to confront Joshua in Joshua 17:3–6 to finally gain their inheritance. Who knows? Maybe these courageous women were friends? (That's one friend group I would have loved to have been a part of!)

The Israelites were preparing to cross the Jordan River to take the Promised Land. The city of Jericho would be their first conquest. Joshua makes a leadership call and as his command is carried out, we meet our study's heroine.

Digging Deeper

Let's start with an overview of this divine appointment that became Rahab's divine assignment.

Begin by reading Joshua 2:1–7. As you read this passage, get to know this brave woman who never lost her poise even amid a fear-filled situation. If this is a familiar story to you, use an online Bible to read the Scripture in a different translation. This little change can make an old story become new!

So far, what can you surmise about Rahab based on these verses?

I wish we had more details about Rahab so that we could know her better. What was her childhood like? Did she feel loved? Did she suffer from abuse? Had she been married at one time? Was she estranged from her family? Was she *forced* to take care of her own needs? What were the details that brought her to a point where prostitution became her profession?

These are questions we don't have the answers to, for the Bible only describes her as "a prostitute whose name was Rahab." Writer Cindy Bultema says, "Too easily we can slip on glasses of judgment instead of grace." We can miss seeing Rahab's humanness if we just read the words that describe her occupation. Yes, she's a woman caught in a snare of sin, a trap maintained by her society. Yet, Rahab was a woman not so unlike you and me, confronted daily with sin's sly pull.

Take a moment and using the questions above, write below some possible answers to Rahab's background that might have contributed to the situation in which the spies found her.

I have never had the opportunity to have a friendship with a woman caught in a place where selling her body seems to be her only means of survival. I have read testimonies, though, and each of these women have had one thing in common: They were not living the life they wanted.

No one *wants* to have her body used time and time again in such a degrading fashion. We were born to be loved, cherished, and adored—at our very core, that is what we desire, crave even. While Rahab is a brave woman, I also see her as a desperate woman. Shoved in a corner with no visible means of escape. Yet God was all the while preparing a way.

Rahab receives a knock at the door, a common occurrence for her.

With her profession, it would have been routine to have visitors; for men to come and go out of Rahab's home. To have some men come in and *not* go out was not.

The men who stayed were two spies from a people known for attacking and obliterating whole countries. These are the men who entered Rahab's home and stayed. I must have watched too many movies because the word *spies* and *staying* made me shudder a bit. Did Rahab tremble when she discovered who she had opened her door to this time?

There doesn't seem to be much discussion, as Rahab lets the men in and quickly moves to find the spies a hiding place. She probably knew it was only a matter of time before another customer would come, so she had to act quickly.

With the spies hidden upstairs, I can only imagine the "what ifs" that played out in Rahab's mind with the pounding of her heart. Write a few possible "what ifs" below:

_____

_____

_____

_____

_____

A few I thought of included:

➤ What if my family finds out and brands me a betrayer?

▶ What if the spies are crueler than most customers, hurting me?

▶ What if the king finds out and I'm tried as a traitor?

▶ What if the spies kill me to keep their secret?

Every time I let my mind go to the "what ifs" in situations that demand my confidence, it doesn't go well. Inevitably, I end up sinking in a hole, imagining every conceivable outcome that rarely, if ever, happens. It has taken me years, but as my confidence in God has grown, I have begun to recognize these defeating thoughts as they appear. I'm learning to not allow them to stay. Though not successful every time, as I partner with the Holy Spirit and His power, I am learning to do what Paul called "taking captive every thought."

Second Corinthians 10:5 says: "We demolish arguments and every pretension that sets itself up against the knowledge of God, and we take captive every thought to make it obedient to Christ." Though not an easy exercise, not allowing defeating thoughts to lodge in our minds is usually the first and most powerful step in making a move toward Spirit-empowered and Spirit-led confidence. When we put down confidence-crushing thoughts, we can pick up Christ Confidence.

> *Putting down confidence-crushing thoughts allows us to pick up Christ Confidence.*

In this verse, the word *argument* in the Greek is *logismos.*[9] Think of our English word *logic.* These thoughts that come rifling through our minds are not silly nor are they impossibilities. That is exactly what makes them so incredibly powerful! The scenarios we worry about can absolutely happen. This is why we have to know God's Word. It is only by faith in the One who can do the impossible, even in the worst circumstances conceivable, that we will conquer these defeating speculations. His Word is the compass, always leading us to True north. He always guides us to the Truth—to Himself.

> *His Word is the compass, always leading us to True north. He always guides us to the Truth—to Himself.*

Rahab began her move toward God on this day when she met the spies. She might not have been aware that she had taken her first step of faith or that she was casting off confidence-defeating thoughts. Despite her past decisions that had stomped on her self worth, she courageously ushered the spies upstairs.

Rahab moved in obedience, and opposition was there to greet her. Someone betrayed her to the king.

Have you ever taken a step of courage, a step of faith, and found opposition coming at you as you did? What was that scenario?

_____

_____

_____

_____

As I shared in week one, my experience in following God's calling is that it has rarely been easy, but it has certainly been adventurous! This is more than true with Rahab.

Joshua 2:3 tells us, "So the king of Jericho sent this message to Rahab: 'Bring out the men who came to you and entered your house, because they have come to spy out the whole land.'"

Who is this Rahab that she receives direct messages from the king of Jericho? Were Rahab and the king on "familiar" terms? Even if Rahab had wanted to make a new path in her life, if the king of Jericho was her customer, how could that have even been possible? Moving toward dignity when the most "dignified" man in the nation treats you with contempt would have *seemed* impossible.

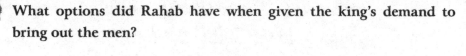

What options did Rahab have when given the king's demand to bring out the men?

_____

_____

Like Rahab, can you think of a time when you have felt you had no choice, that you were backed against a wall? Seeing only the terrifying way out of a situation, we can become paralyzed. We don't have to be! When God is our God, our Father and the Almighty One who possesses all power, we are never without help.

The next verse begins with that powerful word: BUT. One simple word that changes everything. "But the woman had taken the two men and hidden them. She said, 'Yes, the men came to me, but I did not know where they had come from'" (Joshua 2:4).

If Rahab was afraid of the king and getting caught going against his demand, that fear was not as strong as a different motivation.

Continue with Rahab's story by reading Joshua 2:8–24.

What do you think empowered Rahab to defy the authority of the king?

_____

_____

_____

_____

Rahab would not have been in the crowd when Moses read the Ten Commandments many years before nor would she have been a part of the Hebrew feasts that God had created for His people. Being from Jericho, she would not have been included in the promises God had given to the Israelites either. Yet in speaking with the spies, she demonstrates knowledge of their God and the promises He gave to His people.

"We have heard . . . " (Joshua 2:10a), she says.

Stories. How they travel!

Rahab's knowledge of God came to her via another person's story of seeing God at work. She clarifies what the citizens of Jericho have heard, "We have heard how the LORD dried up the water of the Red Sea for you when you came out of Egypt, and what you did to Sihon and Og, the two kings of the Amorites east of the Jordan, whom you completely destroyed" (Joshua 2:10). This account had a profound effect on the people of Jericho: their " . . . hearts melted in fear and everyone's courage failed because of you, for the LORD your God is God in heaven above and on the earth below" (2:11).

Having never seen one of God's miracles for herself, Rahab believed in the power of Israel's God based solely on what she had heard.

Spreading the story is a powerful way for others to be introduced to our Jesus.

Luke 8:26–39 tells the encounter of the demon-possessed man and Jesus, Jehovah-Rapha, our healer. If time permits, read the entirety of this faith-building story.

Looking specifically at Luke 8:38–39, what does Jesus encourage the healed man to do?

_____

_____

Yes, spreading the story is just the way to get out this Good News of the offer of new life. That is exactly what we will see happen in the life of

Rahab: She will receive a new life. Before she will fully understand what that will mean to her, her conditions will become much worse, but she will not lose her poise. Neither will we as we put down confidence-crushing thoughts and pick up Christ Confidence. Leaning on His Word as our compass, we can know He will always lead us to Himself.

Apply It

When it comes to other people seeing God at work in the story of our lives, how would the following people complete this sentence concerning us:

> For our spouse has heard . . .
> For our kids have heard . . .
> For our boss has heard . . .
> For our neighbor has heard . . .
> For our employee has heard . . .
> For our parent has heard . . .

Paul made a point to daily spread his story. He encouraged the believers with these words: "Whatever you have learned or received or heard from me, or seen in me—put it into practice. And the God of peace will be with you" (Philippians 4:9).

Paul knew he was a walking advertisement for a life lived in Christ . . . and a very good one, too.

Spreading *our* story is just as powerful today as the Israelites' and Paul's stories were then.

Finish your time today by writing out your spiritual history—your testimony with God—on an empty page at the back of this book. Keep it short; something you could share in an elevator ride.

Once you have written out this short history, each time you begin a new day of study this week, read your history again. In this way, your testimony will become stored in your heart and mind, where you can quickly retrieve it to share with others. The more times you read it, the more comfortable you will become with it. This step will help you be prepared so you can confidently make your move when the opportunity comes to share your story. (This is how I prepare to speak. I write out my messages and then read them over and over again until I feel comfortable with my content.)

First Peter 3:15 encourages us to do this: "But in your hearts revere Christ as Lord. Always be prepared to give an answer to everyone who asks you to give the reason for the hope that you have. But do this with *gentleness and respect*" (emphasis mine).

Then they will say, "We have heard . . ."

★

A Change in Perspective

MEMORY VERSE: "Now faith is confidence in what we hope for and assurance about what we do not see."—Hebrews 11:1

WHILE THE PEOPLE OF CANAAN had heard of the miracles God had done for the Israelites and "their hearts melted in fear and they no longer had . . . courage" (Joshua 5:1), the same stories fueled Rahab's faith. This was not the first time in the Bible that two people looked at the same situation and reacted two different ways.

Digging Deeper

Let's go back to the beginning of the Israelite's conquest of Canaan in Numbers 13. If you already know the story about the first time spies went into the Promised Land, begin your reading in verse 25. If this history is new to you, get the full account by starting at verse 1.

Initially, upon entering the land, the spies saw God's goodness. How did they describe Canaan in Numbers 13:27?

_____

_____

_____

In the ESV, there is a very powerful conjunction at the beginning of verse 28 that changed everything: *however*. This small word negates every positive thing the ten spies had reported prior to this.

There were two completely different perspectives about the Promised Land within the group of twelve spies. Specifically, how did the ten spies describe the people of the land in verses 26, 31–33?

_____

_____

How did the ten spies describe themselves in verse 33?

_____

_____

Then there is courageous Caleb. Unafraid to go against the norm, he on behalf of himself and Joshua boldly makes his positive perspective known. "Let us go up at once and occupy it, for we are well able to overcome it." (Numbers 13:30 ESV).

What do you think was the reason for these two completely different perspectives?

_____

_____

What role does confidence play in each of these two perspectives?

_____

_____

Twelve spies went into the land. Ten saw defeat. Two saw triumph.

Ten forgot God's promise; they were focused on what they saw, not what God said. They were defeated from the start and so were all those who listened and followed them. They never received God's very best for their lives. Each and every one of them died in the desert, never having reached his potential.

> *Focus on what God says,*
> *not on what you see.*

Jump forward and read Joshua 14:6–15.

What word is used repeatedly to describe the way Caleb followed the Lord (vv. 8–9, 14)? As a result of his faith, and his actions backing up his faith, what did Caleb receive?

_____

_____

_____

_____

The spies of Numbers 13 would have either personally seen or heard about the miracles of the parting of the Red Sea, the pillars of cloud and fire, the provision of manna and quail. Yet, they allowed fear to fuel their hearts instead of faith.

I, too, have had times in my life when my future hung in the balance. Would I see my situation from God's perspective or my own, shortsighted one?

Like many, my heart was broken in a relationship as a young woman. Even today, my heart feels a little pain trigger when I hear another has experienced this same hurt.

I remember questioning: *Why, God? Why* not *this one? Why break up now?*

When God asked me to choose Him over him, my young heart obeyed, but not without a struggle. Lacking history with God, I didn't have His perspective on what my future could hold. My deceived heart told me I was someone because I belonged to someone. God had a different message. He wanted to give me a new perspective so I would know True Love.

Since I had not yet experienced the blessings of obedience, I didn't know many of its benefits. Still, I obeyed God, hoping He knew what He was doing.

He absolutely did. I didn't know all God had to show me or give me at the beginning of this test. Later, as I looked back, I saw how He moved me to a new place where He revealed a side of Himself I hadn't yet experienced. I couldn't experience the full intensity of His love because someone else was occupying that space in my heart. As I leaned into Jesus after the breakup, I began to see what I couldn't see before: just how deep His love for us is.

To learn this, I had to move "out of love" with a boyfriend in order to move "in love" with Jesus. A change in my perspective of the source of true love empowered me to embrace the change in my position.

> *A change in your perspective can empower you to embrace a change in your position.*

God was trying to give the spies His perspective on the land, a place He called "flowing with milk and honey." Yes, taking the land would be difficult, but He would be with them. On the other side of difficult was His very best for them. God was challenging them to believe He could and would deliver on His promises.

Uncomfortable and often painful, the change we fear can be the very thing that moves us toward God's very best for our lives. I saw that very clearly in my life.

Jesus didn't leave me in a position in which I was completely dependent on another person for the love my heart craved. Instead, He moved me to what was a lonely place for a season so He could change the way I understood love. Finding Him to be all my heart craved was the beginning of finding a confidence I would never lose.

Sometimes, God changes our position so we can see things in a fresh way. We have to trust His compass is directing us in the right way.

Please read Matthew 17:1–8.

Where did Jesus lead Peter, James, and John? What significance do you see in the last two words of verse 1?

_____

_____

_____

_____

I see a similarity in their story and mine: Jesus had to move the disciples *away* from others in order for them to see Him in a different light.

Have you had a time in your relationship with Jesus when you sensed Him drawing you to be by yourself or alone for a while? If so, what was the result of that time? How were you changed?

_____

_____

How did God want these disciples' perception of Jesus to change (v. 5)?

_____

_____

Why was it important for them to have this change in perspective going forward?

_____

_____

Jesus led Peter, James, and John for a season to a place not easily accessed. Removing them from familiar places and people was not a punishment but an opportunity. A space in time to get away and gain a new perspective—His perspective. Here, before their very eyes, Jesus' face shone like the sun, and they heard God speak: "This is my Son" (Matthew 17:5a).

When the disciples had a change in their position, they experienced a change in their perspective of Jesus.

To move forward in faith, God may change our position, or we may need to change our perspective. Very often, it is both.

As I read aloud, my three young children were caught up in the far-off land of Narnia. The phone's sudden ring drew us back to Charlotte. "Turn on your TV" was all my friend said before quickly hanging up. In seconds, our screen lit up and we watched smoke swirling above one of the Twin Towers in New York City. The reporter uttered terrifying words: *terrorist attack.* With our little ones huddled close to my side, my mind spun: *I live in a large banking city too. Will ours be next?* There was nothing I could do except wait for the enemy's next move.

Back in Joshua 2, maybe that is what the inhabitants of Jericho were doing the day the spies arrived at Rahab's home. Waiting. Holed up in their homes, hearts melting with fear.

Though her neighbors were "living in terror" (NLT), Rahab chose a different perspective that day. Her safe position as a citizen of the city of Jericho was about to change, but she did not allow herself to cower in fear like her neighbors. Instead, she chose to see by faith and place her courage in a God she had yet to fully encounter.

Rahab trusted God. She believed He was all-powerful and that she could and should rely on Him. She made a decision not to think as others; she chose a redirection. She chose to believe and trust in the God of Israel. This move laid the foundation for a lifetime of trust to come.

Our perspective makes all the difference in how we see a situation. Though Rahab was being removed from all familiar places and people,

God was not punishing her. He was giving her a new opportunity. Rahab changed her perspective and moved forward in faith. God changed her position and, on the other side of difficult, she would find God's very best for her life.

> ## God may allow change in order for us to change.

Though it may be uncomfortable (in fact, at times it is overwhelmingly painful), because of His great love for us, God may use change as His means to create change in us. He knows the potential He has instilled in us and He wants to see that potential come to fruition.

Apply It

God may allow change on the outside in order for us to change on the inside. We may move, change jobs, grow closer or become distanced from loved ones . . . our positions are constantly changing. Each change brings another opportunity for us to change our perspective. Like the disciples, we can see Jesus in ways we haven't before: as our Provider, our Healer, and as our True Love.

Can you identify an area where your position is changing? It may be in your responsibilities as a volunteer, an employee, a mom, a daughter, a wife, or in your calling. We may be moving into positions we have never experienced before and just thinking about it sends a shiver up our spines. Sometimes change can cause our confidence to falter. We can be unsure of whom we are when we are no longer in a comfortable place, maybe in a downright foreign one.

Are you in a season of change? Describe it below. Can you begin to see what changes God might want to make in you through this change?

We can't go back to relationships that have changed, places we've moved on from, or get back things we've given up. Often, we cannot stop the change that is coming in our future. We're on a freeway with no exit. This is our new reality, whether we like it or not.

But in this new place, your loving Father wants to show you His perspective, who *He* is, and what He wants to do in you and through you. Change can be scary and so very uncomfortable. Open your heart past the pain of change and ask God to shift your focus from what is changing to seeing *Him in the change.*

Wrap up your time today by finishing with this prayer:

Lord, often change is painful. Soften my heart to see past this pain and to see Your heart toward me. What I really want isn't always what's best for me. Give me Your perspective. In Jesus' name, Amen.

★

Different

MEMORY VERSE: "Now faith is confidence in what we hope for and assurance about what we do not see."—Hebrews 11:1

EACH DAY seems to have one thing in common. One after another, choices come and demand decisions.

Home decisions hang in the balance. When can I get this fixed? Who will follow through with the repairs? What will it take to get everything done, and how much will it cost?

Work decisions weigh on my mind. What are the next steps to take? Am I the only person who can do this? Do I need to bring in more help? How will this timeline come together?

Relationship decisions tug on my heart. Is "yes" the best answer? When can I spend time with them? Should I really be that honest with my thoughts and feelings?

Decision fatigue.

Even as I write these words, my mind feels so very tired of the many decisions that I need to make. When exhaustion is close, confidence seems so far away.

Most mornings, before I even leave my bed, a prayer seeps from my heart: *Lord, I need Your wisdom.* It's not a giant step of faith, or anything close to that, just an advance in the right direction before the day takes off without me. I have seen time and time again this small step to be exactly what I need before I even know I need it.

So young in her budding faith, Rahab would not have known to breathe a prayer for wisdom as the spies slipped into her home and told her of their mission. Yet upon her deliberate action to honor God, she received exactly what she needed. One prompting after another. God supplied not only the wisdom she needed but also wisdom and specific instruction. *Conceal them on the roof. Use the flax. Exit by a rope. Go through the window. Head to the hills and hide there.*

As Rahab stepped out in belief, wisdom stepped in. God readily gave as she needed. And with movement, prompted by wisdom, her confidence grew.

Digging Deeper

What does James 1:5 instruct us to do?

_____

_____

Without a doubt, this is the verse I quote the most in my life. Ask any friend of mine—if I pray with them, I am going to pray this verse. I know that if there is one thing I need from God and I need to pray for continually, it's wisdom.

Wisdom from God is what Shiphrah and Puah, as well as the daughters of Z needed and received as well.

Rahab's very first step of wisdom was toward the God of the Israelites. She knew, because of His miracles, that He "is God in heaven above and on the earth below" (Joshua 2:11). Rahab's reverence for God moved her toward Him. This choice was more powerful than the fear of the king of Jericho or the fear to simply give up. She knew, from the way God took care of His people, He was a God who cared for those who worshiped Him. The miracles she had heard of, "how the LORD dried up the water of the Red Sea" (v. 10), told the story that God protected His people.

> *As we walk in wisdom, and we see the blessings that come, our confidence builds.*

Rahab needed this confidence as the life she had known would be completely turned upside down.

When I study Scripture, I will often read the same passage over and over again, looking at it from different angles. My friend Leah taught me to simply read the Scripture through the first time just to get an overview. The next time, I read it looking for what I can learn about God and His character. As I read it a third time, I am looking for what God wants to teach me about myself and ways I need to change.

As it turns out, we're going to practice this reading method ourselves! You'll recall that on Day 1, we read Joshua 2. Today, read Joshua 2 from **a different perspective, looking for the answers to these questions: List all the ways Rahab was different from the two spies.**

**List all the ways the spies behaved adversely toward Rahab *because*
she was different from them.**

As I read this passage, I couldn't find one way that the spies treated Rahab any differently than anyone else. The fact that she was a prostitute, a citizen of Jericho, a woman, or a Gentile doesn't seem to come into play in their interaction with her.

Just as God sent the scouts to Rahab, He sends into our lives, our work, our neighborhoods, and churches those who are different from us. Sometimes these people, like Rahab, need Him; they have yet to begin a new life with Him. Other times He sends believers into our lives who are, for various reasons, not the same as us. Different in the way they look. Different on how they interpret minor details of the Bible. We both know Jesus is God's Son, but in other ways, we're just different.

The question is: How do we see each other? Do we extend grace and opportunity like the spies, to get to know those who are not the same as us? Or do we get hung up on "different"?

You might think, "Lynn, what has this got to do with confidence?"

A lot.

When we are truly confident, we are not only comfortable with ourselves, we're comfortable with others. Even people not quite the same as us. On the other hand, when we are insecure, or lack confidence, we're uneasy around those different from us. The uncomfortableness of the unfamiliar rules our thoughts first, then determines our actions. When we are secure in God, we are empowered to show love to all people . . . even our enemies.

My friend Kenisha told me, "Ten years ago, I made a conscious decision to dislike people different from me."

Having just moved to a new city, Kenisha experienced blatant prejudice on a scale she had never experienced before. She grew tired of visiting places where not even the greeters at the front door acknowledged her. Once inside, people either stared right through her or stared her down.

Then one evening as she strolled through her neighborhood, a pickup truck pulled up next to her, someone inside shot a gun off in the air, and several people hurled profanities at her before screeching off into the darkness of the sunset.

As she walked home, wiping away tears and trying to process what happened and why, she made a simple resolve in her heart: *I'm done trying to love these people.* She said she determined—with all the reasoning of a five-year-old in a schoolyard scuffle—*If they don't like me, I won't like them either.*

Once home, she called her mom, told her what happened, and shared her decision to stop caring about the people who had hurt her. Honestly, it was more than just not caring. Kenisha could feel hate taking root in her heart.

Her mother questioned how Kenisha would justify her decision to hate as a follower of Christ.

"I'm glad you're okay, but I can't support your decision." Kenisha's mom challenged her: "You can either continue to be a Christian, to love God and all those He created, or you can decide to go against God and despise His creation . . . but not both. So, which will you choose?"

I didn't say anything about going against God, Kenisha thought, defending her position.

But just as quickly as the thought crossed her mind so did the words of a verse she learned as a child in Sunday school: "So God created mankind in his own image, in the image of God he created them; male and female he created them" (Genesis 1:27).

Up until that point, Kenisha had mostly heard this verse used to describe the sanctity of human life. But now, she was willing to trade this Truth that deemed all human life worthy for the lie that their behavior makes them worthless. The harsh words of her heart were in stark contrast to those Jesus spoke concerning how we are to treat all people, including our enemies.

In what seemed like less than a nanosecond, the same day she decided to hate others turned into the day she decided never to give her heart over to hatred.

Hatred . . . that was a hard word for Kenisha to say. In order to make a conscious decision about why she would always work to steer her heart away from that word, she had to look at that word for all it was.

Turn to Matthew 5. The sermon recorded here demands a lot of us who belong to Christ.

Who does Jesus say are those who "will see God" (v. 8)? How about those who are called the "children of God" (v. 9)?

_____

_____

Jesus goes on, in verses 13 and 14, to give those who are His additional titles. What are they?

_____

_____

Read verses 43–48 and then, looking closely at verse 44, fill in the blanks with the actions Jesus commands us:

"But I say unto you, _____ your enemies, _____ them that curse you, _____ _____ to them that hate you, and _____ for them which despitefully use you, and persecute you" (KJV).

Circle the noun Jesus uses to describe *who* we are to act this way toward.

In verse 47, what actions does Jesus say believers and those yet to believe both do?

_____

_____

So how are we, as followers of Christ, to be different?

_____

_____

Kenisha continued:

> Hate carries a false arrogance that shouts:
> "I'm better than you."
> "I deserve better than you."
> "I wish you would go away."

That's insecurity talking.

At the extreme opposite end of the spectrum, the core of the Christian heart is love. It walks with a humbleness toward others—a gentle knowing that we're all the same at the foot of the cross of Jesus. This kind of love confidently and humbly says:

> *"I'm no better than you."*
> *"All I have I owe to Jesus."*
> *"I'm glad we're here together."*

She is so right! When we know Truth, when Truth is in us and has changed us, we become confident enough to not only love those different from us but even those opposed to us. We can overcome our uncomfortable feelings, love as He loves, and show this world who Jesus really is.

In the movie *Hidden Figures*, Vivian Meredith, a white woman who has repeatedly held Dorothy Vaughn, an African American, from employment advancement, says to Dorothy: "Despite what you think, I don't have anything against y'all." Dorothy simply looks back at Mrs. Meredith and says, "I know *you* probably believe that."[10]

Dorothy could have been saying that to me! As a young woman, I was prejudicial. Oh, I would have never said I was because I didn't know I was. Sometimes you don't know what you don't know! Growing up in a small, sheltered town, I looked down on *any* person different from me and any situation different from mine.

In this same chapter, Matthew 5, look at verse 19 to see what Jesus has to say about breaking the commands He gives us.

Matthew 5 wraps up with some very powerful, and possibly misconstrued words of Jesus. Write out Matthew 5:48 below.

Does the word *perfect* do to you what it once did to me? Talk about stripping you of all confidence! Jesus, the Son of God, is telling us to be perfect?

Here's one of those times when doing a little word study is imperative. The word *perfect* here in the Greek is *teleios*, meaning "perfect, mature, finished."[11]

If there is anything that can wipe out our insecurities and self-doubt, it is when we allow the Holy Spirit to do His work in us, making us mature. That is, finishing the good work that God has already started in us.

If we don't submit to this work, we're the ones who are going to miss out. Miss out on the discovery of diversity and all the beauty there is to see and experience in *different*! But not only are we going to miss out, we will be disobeying Christ's command to love our neighbor and our enemy.

As we walk in wisdom, humility, and love, we will see the blessings that come, and our confidence will build. Our deliberate actions to honor God will put us in a position where, like Rahab, we can receive exactly what we need in each and every situation.

Apply It

Take a moment to think back over your upbringing. How have your experiences impacted the way you do or do not love others? Ask the Holy Spirit to open your eyes to how you have loved others. Maybe like me, there is prejudice lurking in your heart that you never knew was there.

Take a moment to bravely pray and ask the Holy Spirit to bring into your life those who are different from you and to build into you a confidence that overcomes uncomfortable.

Lord, it sure is easy to stick to spending time with people who are like me. Challenge me, Lord. Open my eyes to see people, all different types of people, and teach me to love as You love. In Jesus' name, Amen.

★

The Duel with Doubt and Wait

MEMORY VERSE: "Now faith is confidence in what we hope for and assurance about what we do not see."—Hebrews 11:1

ALL TOO OFTEN, as soon as we step out, doubt steps in.

"Doubt on an emotional level is indecision between belief and disbelief. Doubt involves uncertainty, distrust or lack of sureness of an alleged fact, an action, a motive, or a decision."[12]

The definition itself is the opposite of confidence. Just reading it conjures up strong emotions in my heart. I have experienced the power of doubt. I know the feeling of hanging in the balance between belief and disbelief. *I believe you, God. Well, at least I want to believe you, but sometimes I don't.* And when I don't, I feel horrible; like I have disappointed Him so much.

I probably shouldn't admit this here, in the middle of a Bible study of all things, but have you ever had that weird feeling come over you: *What am I doing? What if He isn't real?*

As I said, I probably shouldn't say that here of all places, but honestly, this doubt cloud just came over me last week on a walk. There I was, strolling down the street, talking to Jesus, when the thought popped in my head: *What if I am making this whole thing up?* (It's a good thing Jesus says in Jude 1:22 to have mercy on those who doubt!)

For years, I have been trying to identify thoughts that are toxic to my faith. I know I cannot give doubt any oxygen to breathe. Though I can't touch faith or wrap my arms around my Jesus, He is what I *hope* for. He is where my confidence is, and I *choose* to *fully trust, believe in the powers, trustworthiness, and reliability of Christ*. So, I made a choice to not give the doubting thoughts space in my mind and replaced them with God's Word that I have made a point to remember.

That is not to say we don't or won't ever experience doubt. Clearly, I do; and I bet you do too. The thought that pops in our minds is not sin; we can't stop it from happening. Our response to it is what matters. Whether we have faith and become confident, though, has everything to do with what we *do* with the doubt. Does it get to stay in our minds? Hang out? Grow a bit until it is a full-on faith crisis?

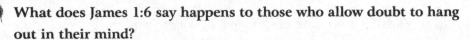

What does James 1:6 say happens to those who allow doubt to hang out in their mind?

Just the image of what this verse portrays wearies me. So does doubt. It beats us around and around a boxing ring. Belief. Disbelief. Belief. Disbelief. We have to train daily in order to strengthen and stabilize our faith and stop doubt. We do that by reading the Truth in His Word and continually carrying on conversational prayer. Maybe at times it's phoning a friend who can hear our doubts and struggles and won't freak out. A friend who will listen and then give us the "what for" (in a very loving way, of course!).

Rahab didn't have the Bible. She didn't have a church, a small group, or Bible study. (If you don't have one either, ask a friend about the church they attend and join us at Proverbs 31 Ministries for studying God's Word together!)

Rahab didn't have the Word of God at her fingertips, like you and I, as she may have wondered: *Will the spies keep their promise? Will I be caught and tried? Is this God for real, or am I jeopardizing my whole life on a story I heard?*

She did have the red cord.

Every day, as long as she left it hanging from her window, Rahab would have seen the red cord.

To tell you the truth, just the sight of red can sometimes make me pass out, especially if it's blood coming out of one I love. Something tells me I shouldn't go into all my stories of my husband and my kids and their accidents . . . and me passed out on the ground.

The color of Rahab's cord, blood red, was no coincidence. The red cord was her saving grace, the same color as the blood that one day would save us all.

This red cord would have been a daily reminder of the promise she was given—a symbol.

The Bible is full of symbols. Let's look at a few less familiar ones.

What does white hair represent in God's Word? See Daniel 7:9 and Revelation 1:14.

_____

_____

How about rocks? Read Psalm 18:2 and Psalm 40:2.

_____

_____

And fire in Acts 2:3?

_____

_____

Symbols can be powerful reminders, bolstering our faith just when we need a boost.

One day last year, I felt so strongly the struggle—no, the wrestling—that comes when we choose to walk with the Lord and contrary to this world. I knew I needed something: a symbol, a sign that would serve as a declaration. That very day I ordered a sign, a huge sign, that reads, "But as for me and my house, we will serve the LORD" (KJV). Joshua's declaration in Joshua 24:15 now hangs above our kitchen table. Right where we gather, it is a constant reminder: No matter what life looks like or what is going on around me today, we will serve the Lord!

That may have been the power Rahab experienced when she looked at the red cord: *I am going to leave behind this deplorable life, and I will serve Israel's God.*

The day for the red cord's use had finally arrived. Rahab felt her heart pounding when she saw the people coming. So very many people.

<u>Read Joshua 6:1–23 for the account of the day.</u>

Since she lived on the wall (Joshua 2:15), Rahab would have been an eyewitness to the mysterious, ominous daily marches of the Israelites. What might have gone through her mind and heart as she watched from her wall window?

She was stuck. Her situation was dire and held the potential for death. Everyone in the city knew it: "Now the gates of Jericho were securely barred because of the Israelites. No one went out and no one came in" (Joshua 6:1).

As Rahab's deliverance drew closer, so did the clamor (Joshua 6:8–9). There is a reason people say, "It has to get worse before it gets better." The noise and unrest grew and grew with the marching feet of silent, armed men, the continual blowing of horns, and a mysterious, ornate box followed by more silent, armed men.

What was going to happen? When was it going to happen?

In Joshua 2:18–20, how much information had the spies given Rahab concerning what she could expect when the Israelites took Jericho?

_____

_____

Rahab was only given her *next* move.

Yes, while all hell was literally breaking loose, Rahab had to wait. While she stayed still, she had no way of knowing the outcome developing outside. As stones crumbled, her home and all she knew fell apart. She had a choice to make. She could let anxiety take over and run, or she could hold onto the Israelites' promise and wait.

Have you ever been in a situation which required a massive amount of faith and, as you waited for God to move, your situation only seemed to worsen? How did you respond to the wait?

_____

_____

_____

I am in that situation right now. I need God to make His move. I trust and believe He will, but as I wait, the tension increases. At times, the weight of waiting is demoralizing. Yet, like Rahab, I have my instructions.

Pray.

Believe.

Have faith that the Lord will see me through.

Sometimes, friend, the right move to make is no move at all.

Sometimes the right move is no move at all.

As we read earlier in Luke 9:28–36, the story of the Transfiguration, the right move for the disciples was no move, and they missed it. Excitement, impulse, maybe anxiousness pushed Peter, and he took action. Lack of understanding and foolishness made the disciples think a move would be good. They didn't understand what the time and place were for. It was the wrong time for action; it was time to be still.

Jesus didn't rebuke the disciples. God's own words, "This is my Son, whom I have chosen; listen to him" (Luke 9:35) did it all. His voice showed the disciples what it was time for. Waiting. Listening. Unfortunately, before they knew it, the moment had passed. The disciples had missed experiencing the peace and powerful presence of God Himself.

In our lives, there are different seasons. Times to move, times to wait, and times to get out of God's way. Let's follow Rahab's lead and not let anxious or doubtful thoughts take over and drive us to *do* something. Instead, let's rest confidently, waiting for God's instruction, and listen for the voice of wisdom.

Apply It

In what season of faith are you currently? Time for movement? Time for waiting? Time for getting out of God's way?

Like the disciples, it isn't always as clear as it was for Rahab. We need wisdom from the Holy Spirit and a revelation from God to know the season we are in.

Take a few moments to be still today, asking the Holy Spirit to reveal to you what season of faith you are in. Ask Him to give you the wisdom, strength, and discipline to meet Him there.

★

When the Blessing Comes

MEMORY VERSE: "Now faith is confidence in what we hope for and assurance about what we do not see."—Hebrews 11:1

WHEN RAHAB CHOSE TO STAY in her home while her community crumbled outside her door, she was in fact taking a step of faith. One after another, her steps of faith took her closer and closer to reaching the potential Christ instilled in her. As she heard the scuffling, shouting, and ransacking of her city, she believed, before she received, that God would prove faithful.

Digging Deeper

Let's review what we read yesterday by looking again at Joshua 6, this time reading up to verse 25. As you read, note below how many times Rahab's name is mentioned in this chapter.

Look closely at the second sentence of verse 17. How does Rahab's actions and our memory verse of Hebrews 11:1 fit together?

_____

_____

_____

_____

As I read the whole of Rahab's story, I didn't see any specific prayer she prayed or action she took that describes the exact time and place that Rahab made the move from idol worship to Yahweh worship. Her story of salvation reminds me of a friend of mine.

Colleen invited me to lunch at her home after meeting me for the first time at church. Since we had never spent time together before, in making conversation I asked her when she began her new life in Christ.

She couldn't give me a direct answer.

I tried not to look shocked. Growing up, I had been taught you needed to have a definitive moment when you said _the_ prayer or walked down the aisle at church.

She didn't.

In her late teens, Colleen started hearing Christian music and began believing the words she heard. Then she went to church and started believing what they taught. Next, she set out to read the Bible and she accepted what she read. It was a gradual process to where she was now: a strong woman of God sharing her faith in very powerful ways.

I found it amazing . . . and refreshing! God didn't always begin a relationship with people the way I had been taught that He did, and I found that to be very cool.

Steps of faith, one after another, is what brought both these women to the place where God was the Lord of their lives.

Rahab continued to take these brave steps, even after her rescue.

After Rahab and her family were rescued from Jericho, what does Joshua 6:23 tell us took place?

_____

_____

_____

In Joshua 6, do you see any indication of whether or not she stayed there?

_____

_____

My heart gets so excited when I see verse 25, because we can see, based on Rahab's actions, her faith in God grew. When the Israelites came to save her, they took her family outside the camp, but verse 25 tells us "she lives among the Israelites to this day."

At some point, Rahab moved inside the Israelite camp. Inside the camp, she would never have been able to practice her sinful way of meeting her own needs. Away from self-reliance and toward God-reliance, she found Him to be her need-meeter; her everything. Rahab finally found her heart at home in Him.

Jumping to the next time Rahab is mentioned in the Bible, we can see she continued to experience God's goodness after her deliverance from the destruction of Jericho.

Read Matthew 1:1–6, looking for Rahab's name. What's the context?

_____

_____

_____

I cannot even fathom an honor of this magnitude. No longer Rahab the Prostitute; she was Rahab the grandmother of King David!

Continue reading through this genealogy in Matthew 6 to verse 16. Whose beautiful name does this family line end with?

_____

_____

As Rahab took those beginning steps of courage the day she opened the door to the spies, she could have never foreseen the majestic doors that would open in her future. Because of her brave obedience, she would one day become the wife of one of the spies, Salmon. "Salmon was a prince of the house of Judah, and thus, Rahab, the one-time heathen harlot, married into one of the leading families of Israel and became an ancestress of our Lord."[13]

Both Christians and Jews have tried to say that the Rahab listed here in Christ's genealogy is not the Rahab of Jericho. The fact that a harlot could possibly be included in the line of David, let alone the line of Christ, is disgusting to them. But even if this were so (which research proves it is not), Jesus' heritage includes others who *had* sin-filled stories as well. Not just the stories of Tamar and Bathsheba, but men's stories of sin: Jacob, King David, Solomon, and many others. A look at the Old Testament accounts of their lives highlight not just their walks of faith but their footsteps of failure too.

God obviously uses imperfect people before, during, and in the middle of their process.

The Bible is straightforward about Rahab's work: "So they went and entered the house of a prostitute named Rahab and stayed there" (Joshua 2:1b). Rahab was used by God not because of her profession but in spite of her profession. Notice that the wording used is present tense; Rahab was *still* working when God caused her path to intersect with the spies. Rahab was not given the opportunity to exercise her faith *after* she renounced her lifestyle. She was currently working as a prostitute when she was given the opportunity to partner with God.

See God's hand of grace here? God could have picked anyone to be the point of connection for the spies. There are several stories in the Bible of men and women who served God even though they lived in an idolatrous land. Just look at Lot and Joseph. Yet, God handpicked Rahab. God picked a prostitute.

God moves in His way and sometimes we just need to get out of the way!

> ## God moves in His way and sometimes we just need to get out of the way!

When Rahab offered her help to the spies, their reply wasn't, "Oh, no, thank you. This is God's plan, and He would not choose someone like you to be a part of it." The fact that God used imperfect Rahab is proof He doesn't need perfect people to fulfill His perfect plan. (It's a good thing because I wouldn't stand a chance of being used!)

> ## God doesn't need perfect people to fulfill His perfect plan.

From Rahab's life, we can grasp hold of this truth: God can and will use us *as* we are in process. God is more than capable of drawing us into His will and plan even as our faith is budding, if we will only be drawn.

In fact, He is so very merciful, He says in Isaiah 65:1, "I revealed myself to those who did not ask for me; I was found by those who did not seek me. To a nation that did not call on my name, I said, 'Here am I, here am I.'" Hear Him doing the drawing? All we have to say is yes.

When Rahab said to the spies, "I know that the LORD has given you this land . . . the LORD your God is God in heaven above and on the earth below" (Joshua 2:9, 11), this was very likely the first time she had ever voiced her belief. This was her yes even as God was already using her.

We may put boundaries and barriers around who God uses, including ourselves. God is not as shortsighted as we are. He sees who we are and who He has created us to become. When we are in process, He already sees our future! Rahab may have worn the label of prostitute from her own people and sinner and Gentile by the Hebrews, but the woman God saw was the woman she was becoming and would one day fully be: Rahab, confident woman of faith.

Not only does this strengthen my faith for me, it encourages me to keep praying for those who are not seeking Him yet!

Faith. That is what God looks at. He looks for a heart that is pursuing Him, trusting in Him, and putting that faith into action. He is less about the perfect and more about the pursuit. Though Rahab knew little about Him, what she knew, she was going after.

> *God is less about our perfection and more about our pursuit.*

Rahab was chosen, handpicked, and selected by God to "go and bear fruit" that would last (see John 15:16). What was her lasting fruit? Please read Hebrews 11:31 for the answer.

_____

_____

This means there is hope for you and me! The poor choices of my past and the poor choices I've made in the past twenty-four hours do not exclude me from being used by Jesus. Because of the forgiveness offered and received from our Savior, we can rise again and embrace that His mercies are new every morning, emphasis on *every* (Lamentations 3:22–23)!

This foundation of grace and mercy is the unshakable foundation on which we can build our confidence. A grace and mercy not dependent on what I did yesterday or what I will do today. If we get our choices right or we get them wrong, His choice stays the same: you and me. Yes, He has chosen us. It is done, completed. Over with. He is not going to renege or regret His choice to choose us.

How can we be so sure?

Turn to John 15:16. Write below the very words Jesus spoke when He was on the earth.

_____

_____

Circle the word that describes who did the choosing. Underline the part of the verse that describes why He did this choosing. Jesus ends this powerful verse with an invitation to us. What is it?

_____

_____

What limitations does He put on this invitation?

_____

_____

All too often, confidence, or our lack of it, comes into play when it comes to the things we ask the Father for. Doubt squeezes our faith, pushing us to discouragement that the desires of our hearts will ever come to pass. Sometimes that discouragement leads to desperation and on to despair.

What is the one thing in your life that you need the confidence and the faith to ask the Father for in the name of Jesus?

_____

_____

_____

Grab hold of faith today by soaking in the whole of Rahab's story. If God can take a harlot and make her part of the heritage of the Son of God, He can do anything for you! It may just be a matter of time.

How old was Rahab when the spies came to her door? How old was she when she married Salmon and gave birth to Boaz? We don't know. Maybe like other Old Testament women such as Sarah, Rachel, or Hannah, her wait was long and painful. I know the thing that I pray daily for and continue to trust Him for has reached that pain-filled place in my heart. Today, I choose to believe Hebrews 11:1: "Now faith is confidence in what we hope for and assurance about what we do not see." I am choosing to have confidence in what I hope for and Who my hope is in: the author of this promise, Jesus. I have an assurance so deep in my soul, it settles me. Faith pushes back the darkness of doubt so I can anticipate the answer on the horizon. This confidence is the compass that keeps pointing me forward, to the time and the day this cry of my heart *is* answered. Even as I type, my heart just wants to pre-celebrate the very day of this discovery; God has answered my prayer.

But what about now? What about this balance we hang in? This place between the now and the not yet?

The Bible isn't done teaching us through the life of Rahab. Read James 2:14–26. In verse 19, why does James say it is not enough to simply believe?

_____

_____

After his praise of Rahab, what bold proclamation does James make in wrapping up this important passage?

_____

_____

Rahab had faith _and_ she demonstrated faith. She _did_ something. The doing is what gives life to our faith. It is what turns our supplications into stories.

Shiprah and Puah defied Pharaoh and delivered the babies. They let them live.

Jochebed and Miriam saved Moses. They put him in the basket.

The daughters of Zelophehad asked for the land. They went a second time and asked again (Joshua 17:3–6).

Rahab opened the door. She hid the spies. She left the red rope hanging. She stayed in her shelter. She left all she knew to become someone new.

Faith. Confident faith. It is what each one demonstrated. Never _knowing_ the outcome, they were sure of what they hoped for. They were certain of what they could not see.

Certain that God was faithful.

Certain that God was God. He was and is:

➤ _Jehovah Nissi,_ who stood guard over them;

➤ _Jehovah Jireh,_ their provider;

➤ _El Elyon,_ the One who is exalted above all others;

➤ _Abba,_ the One who was their Father.[14]

They put their faith to work and so shall we.

Like those who have gone before us, we will put our faith to work. It will not be dead. Rahab believed, before she received, that God would prove faithful. He was! God proved to her, and to us, that He uses imperfect people before, during, and in the middle of our process. Now it's time to step out in faith!

127

Apply It

Fear and failure both could have held back Rahab, but they did not.

Friend, where does your faith need to make a move today?

Does that move pertain to the prayer you mentioned above?

Take a moment, shut your book and shut your eyes. Get quiet. Ask the Holy Spirit: What is my faith-move? What is my step of faith, taken in Your confidence, that You want to empower me for today?

Group Discussion Questions

Read this week's memory verse aloud as a group, or select an individual to do so: "Now faith is confidence in what we hope for and assurance about what we do not see."—Hebrews 11:1

1. Share a current situation in your life where you need to have faith—a hope and an assurance for something that you do not yet see.

2. "Sometimes our confidence can falter when God seems elusive" (Lynn Cowell). *Elusive* means "difficult to find, evasive." Do you think there would be a time when God might be elusive on purpose? When might Rahab have felt this?

3. How do you follow God when you feel like you can't hear or see Him? How do you keep going after Him when the boost you need, to know He's helping you, doesn't come?

4. "When I don't know if I should move, it is awfully hard to make a move." When we feel stuck in the decision-making process or we lack the wisdom and confidence we need to make a decision, what could be our first move to see if we're going in the right direction?

5. Rahab, knowing very little about this Israelite God, took one brave step: she hid the spies. Share a situation in your life in which you sense God might be nudging you to move, but you're not quite sure. Share what your brave step might be.

Read together Joshua 6:20–21. Rahab may not have *felt* confident, but her actions portrayed confidence.

Wrap up your time together today by asking the Holy Spirit to empower you to maintain your confidence in Him and His promises, even when, and most often when, He feels elusive.

Deborah

WHEN CONFIDENCE IS REQUIRED

★

PRAYER: *Lord, as we begin this new week, give us fresh eyes. Through the life of Deborah and her calling, empower us to see our own calling and to confidently take Your hand and follow. In Jesus' name, Amen.*

MEMORY VERSE: "'So may all your enemies perish, LORD! But may all who love you be like the sun when it rises in its strength.' Then the land had peace forty years."—Judges 5:31

DAY ONE

★

I Pick You

WHEN IT COMES TO SPEAKING, my normal situation involves a Friday or Saturday spent investing in women, girls, or both. Normal is not a Sunday morning speaking to a congregation of women *and* men.

Yet, I had received a call.

A church asked if a Proverbs 31 Ministries speaker would give the message for "Ladies' Day." This was a special Sunday morning when the women of their church prepared the whole service, and they wanted a woman to deliver the Sunday morning message as well. As one of the few Proverbs 31 Ministries speakers who is comfortable speaking to both men and women, our speaking coordinator asked me to go.

After talking it over with my husband, I said yes.

Weeks later, on a Saturday, my daughters and I made the four-hour trip to the town where the church is located. Waking early the next morning, I slipped on the new dress I had chosen for the occasion. Looking in the full-length mirror, I thought, *How did this dress get so short?* When I bought it, it seemed perfect. Now, looking at my reflection, I imagined myself very soon on a platform in front of a mixed audience. Sick to my stomach, my confidence was slipping. With no backup outfit, what was I to do?

I asked my girls to be part of my solution. After dropping me off at the church, they needed to locate some leggings—stat.

Entering the church foyer, I was greeted by the planner of this special day. She had done a much better job of dressing for the occasion. My self-esteem continued to slip as thoughts swirled in my head. *Just look at her. She looks like she's the one speaking today. Why couldn't you have dressed like her?* As I let her know my daughters were off to find me proper attire, I contemplated, *Maybe I'll hide out in the bathroom until they get back from the store.*

As soon as the girls returned from the store and my leggings were in place, I slid behind the pastor in the second row, waiting for my time to step up. (Can I just tell you that even as I am typing this story my stomach is still doing flip-flops!)

The pastor, dressed in a smart suit, began his introduction: "How many of you have heard of Lynn Cowell?" *No one has heard of Lynn Cowell. Why did he say that?* my mind questioned as my heart started pounding more than usual. "I have enjoyed listening to her on the radio for years," he continued. *Oh no! He thinks I'm the president of Proverbs 31 Ministries, Lysa TerKeurst.* (In many parts of America, Lysa is a well-known speaker and author, who has been ministering to women for many years.) My face must have shown my horror because he looked at me and said, "It is Proverbs 31 Ministries, right?" I bobbed my head up and down, unable to articulate a response. *Yes, I am definitely part of Proverbs 31 Ministries, but I am not who he thinks I am! What should I do? I can't correct him in front of his congregation.* Before I could comprehend what was happening, he called me up to speak.

And that was the start of my Sunday morning.

Talk about losing your confidence! I felt so profoundly out of place.

We each have different gifts, talents, and callings. I am simply a woman doing the assignments God gives to *me*. I work, each day, with the Holy Spirit to be confident where He places me. (Some days it is more of a struggle than others!) This is the confidence I needed to hold on to as I walked onto the stage, whispering under my breath, *Lord, help me!*

I imagine Deborah could have whispered this prayer as well.

The book of Judges, where Deborah's story is told, is believed to be written by Samuel, the last of the judges. During this time, God told the Israelites *He Himself* was their king. Though the surrounding countries had human kings, God told Israel He was enough for them. He did, however, set in place persons who would act as His spokesman and, at times, settle disputes. There were a total of fifteen judges over a span of about 325 years.

The judges God appointed were always men with the exception of one extraordinary woman.

You and I have so much to learn about walking confidently in our calling from Deborah, Israel's fourth judge.

Digging Deeper

Please read Deborah's story in Judges 4.

Judges 4:1 begins by setting the backdrop, "Again the Israelites did evil in the eyes of the LORD." Cold toward God, the Israelites "again" chose their way against God's.

This is not the first time the Bible records such a description of God's people. Earlier in this same book, Judges 3:7 (ESV) tells us, "And the people of Israel did what was evil in the sight of the LORD. They forgot the LORD their God and served the Baals and the Asheroth."

So like us, the Israelites were easily distracted. Their cravings cried out for a physical god they could touch, see, and smell. They wanted what the other countries had: a god they could carry into war. Yet no matter how hard they sprinted from Jehovah, they never found what they were looking for in the other direction. Every time they ran, their cravings only created more captivity.

In this oppressing climate, we are introduced to our next mentor, Deborah. The judge most committed to honoring God and following His ways explicitly, her obedience prepared her for the unique work God had gifted her for.

What does Judges 4:4 mention as Deborah's first role?

_____

_____

Prophets are those who, compelled by God's Spirit, deliver messages to the people in God's name. They are God's authorized spokesmen or speakers.[15] We read earlier that Miriam, Moses's sister, was also a prophet. Prophecy is one of the spiritual gifts.

Read 1 Corinthians 12:1–11.

Paul begins his explanation of spiritual gifts in verse 1 stating, "I do not want you to be uninformed." I don't want to be uninformed either!

Paul explains there are a variety of gifts, services, and activities, but they all come from our triune God.

Many spiritual gifts are listed in this passage, but the purpose for them is all the same. What is that purpose according to verse 7?

_____

_____

_____

_____

Every one of us has at least one spiritual gift. Sometimes our spiritual gifts are obvious. But other times, they not as clear. If so, pray and ask the Holy Spirit to reveal to you your gift or gifts. In addition to this time with the Holy Spirit, you can also purchase books specifically on this topic. Many even include a simple test to help you discover your gifts. Free online resources are available too; just do an internet search using the words "spiritual gifts test."

In this passage, Paul compares the church to our physical body. Each part has an important, but different, function. Like our human body, *every* part is vital to the existence of it. (We've just got to see that!)

First Corinthians 12:18 tells us, "But in fact God has placed the parts in the body, every one of them, just as he wanted them to be." God reassures us that He knew exactly what He was doing when He created us, giving each of us the particular gifts He has chosen for us to fulfill His purpose.

Knowing our spiritual gift(s) is an important block in building our confidence. Knowing and then using our spiritual gifts reassures us of our purpose and place in God's plan.

> *Knowing and living out our spiritual gifts builds confidence as we understand our purpose and place in God's plan.*

Have you come to recognize the spiritual gifts God has given you? If so, what are they?

_____

_____

_____

To know that we belong, that we have a place, is a universal craving. When we know and begin using our spiritual gifts for "the common good," as Paul calls it, we increase our understanding that we belong. The body of Christ is the place God designed for each and every one of us to have a place where that longing to contribute can be fulfilled. When we know, deep in the places that no one sees, that we belong and have a purpose, we can say no to the urge to compare. Because when I know what God has called *me* to, I can more easily celebrate what God has called *you* to. There is no reason for me to compare myself to you. We're simply different, and our diversity is a beautiful thing!

> *When I know what God has called me to,*
> *I can celebrate what God has called you to.*

Yes, some spiritual gifts get more applause than others. We can do our part, though, to safeguard the church from lifting up other brothers and sisters to a place God never intended them to be elevated. We must not confuse gifts on the forefront for gifts that are foremost. One gift is not more important than another. I learned this on Sunday mornings at 5:30 a.m.

As the rooster crowed, Greg and I would climb out of our car and make our way to the high school every other Sunday morning. (What a rooster was doing crowing in the middle of a major metropolitan city, I have no idea, but that's another thing entirely.) The rooster's noisy welcome always reminded me that Greg and I were up working before most people were considering moving.

The big box trucks already in place were evidence that another team had begun serving even before we did. It was time for us to turn the public school into a sanctuary. Being a part of a "portable church," our congregation rented a local high school each week to meet. Our team, the set-up crew, did everything we could to try to change the atmosphere from academic to worshipful each week. Hanging drapes, setting up chairs, and transforming classrooms into children's church rooms were all part of our volunteer description.

Most mornings, I was happy to be serving with my man. This type of physical work was a welcome change from the type of roles we each played during the week.

Other mornings, when my alarm went off at 4:45 a.m., my thoughts were not that positive. *Sundays are for rest, so why am I not resting?* And still other times it wasn't my alarm tempting me to take my thoughts in the wrong direction. Hearing an invitation to a leaders' meeting we were not a part of, or others receiving visible recognition, would try to root discontentment or jealousy in my mind. *Greg and I have so many other talents and gifts that our church doesn't know about. We're serving when others are sleeping. It's like we're invisible.* I knew my thoughts didn't come from a good place. For sure it wasn't the Holy Spirit telling me I needed to be seen! Those on my team had no idea that right there in that high school cafeteria, the enemy and I were having a knock-down brawl most weeks as I fought not to allow these thoughts any space in my mind and heart. I couldn't stay caught in comparison because I knew if I did I would keep right on going all the way to resentment.

Comparison is a one-way road to resentment.

I knew in my head that the service Greg and I provided at church was *not* less important just because it was less visible. Paul's words make this clear: "The parts of the body that seem to be weaker are indispensable" (1 Corinthians 12:22 ESV). He lets us know that comparison and competition have no place in the church. But we know that the battle against comparison is real!

Two of my gifts are serving and teaching. Your gifts are probably different than mine. While I might have the gift of teaching, you're probably way better at hospitality, praying, or leading worship. The difference is how we see the gifts we *do* have rather than what we *don't* have. Jesus gives us these gifts, and we have each been given gifts simply because we belong to Jesus. "But as it is, God arranged the members in the body, each one of them, as he chose" (1 Corinthians 12:18 ESV). We need to see the gifts God has given us as our assets rather than allowing comparison to call out our deficits.

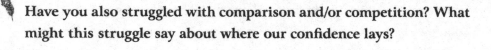

See the gifts God has given you as your assets rather than allowing comparison to call out your deficits.

Have you also struggled with comparison and/or competition? What might this struggle say about where our confidence lays?

_____

_____

Competition and comparison destroy the common good Paul speaks of in 1 Corinthians 12:7. *Common good* used in 1 Corinthians 12:7 is the Greek word *symphero*, meaning "to bring together, to be helpful, be gained."[16] When we all bring our different, unique, not-one-gift-is-quite-like-mine to the body of Christ, we bring together what is helpful to all—we all gain. This is why we must guard our hearts. We must not allow room for the enemy to use *us* to break up the body of Christ. The enemy would love nothing more than to use what was meant to pull us together to pull us apart. Not only that, when we contrast our gift with another's, we are telling God we don't approve; He got it wrong.

Proverbs 27:17 gives us the solution: "As iron sharpens iron, so one person sharpens another." We have the power to turn the enemy's plan for dissension into our own personal growth plan; we can learn from each other.

Do you know of someone who has the same spiritual gift as you and has developed it? How can you learn from that person?

_____

_____

_____

As we review the gifts Paul lists in 1 Corinthians 12, we come to prophecy, Deborah's particular gift. One of only four female prophets for the Lord mentioned in the Bible, Deborah used her gift in her interactions with Barak, the commander of Israel's army.

Why do you think God gave the gift of prophecy to Deborah at a time when her countrymen had been running from Him?

There is no doubt there would have been plenty of opposition to Deborah's leadership; some would have thought her an "inappropriate" leader as a woman. Could God possibly have chosen Deborah for the sheer purpose of drawing attention to His greatness and for the common good of His people?

Bible commentator Matthew Henry describes Deborah's relationship with God: "That she was intimately acquainted with God; she was *a prophetess*, one that was instructed in divine knowledge by the immediate inspiration of the Spirit of God, and had gifts of wisdom, to which she attained not in an ordinary way: she *heard the words of God*, and probably *saw the visions of the Almighty*."[17]

Tough environments for our assignments can condition us to build our confidence on Christ alone. Deborah knew the source of her strength. She wasn't leading others on her own. Instead, she fully relied on the supernatural strength God provided to take on an unlikely assignment.

Knowing and living out our spiritual gifts builds confidence as we understand our purpose and place in God's plan. Then, when I know what God has called me to, I can celebrate what God has called you to. I can rest assured that when God gave me the gifts He gave me, He knew exactly what He was doing. He will use the right circumstances and environment for my gifts so that I can build my confidence on Christ alone.

Apply It

As you think of the gifts and talents God has given you, are you using these to bring together the body of Christ, to help us all to gain in God's kingdom?

_____

_____

List three ways you can position yourself to say yes to God and use the gifts He has given you.

➤ _____

➤ _____

➤ _____

If you haven't already, carve out some time over the next couple of days to take a spiritual gifts test. (It doesn't take very long!)

★

Send the Help

MEMORY VERSE: "'So may all your enemies perish, LORD! But may all who love you be like the sun when it rises in its strength.' Then the land had peace forty years."—Judges 5:31

NOT ONLY WAS BEING A WOMAN IN LEADERSHIP outside the norm in the Old Testament, but as we'll see in Deborah's story, she was also the only female to fill a military leadership role. Just because this was not God's usual choice, there is nothing in Scripture that indicates she was chosen by God because no man would step up to the plate. There are also no details that would lead us to believe Deborah was God's second choice. Instead, her leadership is a historical picture of Galatians 3:28 displayed: "There is neither Jew nor Gentile, neither slave nor free, nor is there male and female, for you are all one in Christ Jesus."

What has been your experience when it comes to equality in the body of Christ?

_____

_____

_____

_____

Has this experience impacted your own personal level of confidence, especially as it pertains to being used by God?

_____

_____

_____

_____

Many of us women have had experiences in the church that have caused us to question our callings as well as our place in the body of Christ. I think this is one reason it is so important for us to take the time to really study the women of the Bible and understand the women God has used in the past. They can help us to see God is for women!

Another of Deborah's God-appointed roles is described in Judges 4:4–5—judging Israel. According to verse 5, Deborah's "courtroom" was open-air: "She held court under the Palm of Deborah." Here the Israelites came to have their disputes decided.

Deborah was responsible for bringing God's justice to the Israelites. Justice is very important to the Lord. Isaiah 30:18 reveals His passionate heart: "Yet the LORD longs to be gracious to you; therefore he will rise up to show you compassion. For the LORD is a God of justice. Blessed are all who wait for him!" Not only does He value justice, it is *who* He is. God *is* just.

Many examples of the importance of justice are modeled in God's Word. Abraham, knowing God's heart for justice, uses his knowledge as part of the case he built trying to save Sodom and Gomorrah from destruction: "Far be it from you to do such a thing—to kill the righteous with the wicked, treating the righteous and the wicked alike. Far be it from you! Will not the Judge of all the earth do right?" (Genesis 18:25).

David extolled God for his love of justice: "For the LORD loves the just and will not forsake his faithful ones" (Psalm 37:28).

Not only does God love justice, He wants His people to love justice as well.

Let's look at what my Bible calls "The Hall of Faith" by reading Hebrews 11:33–34. Who are those who "administered justice" listed alongside?

_____

_____

What does this list of extraordinary acts done by God's people say about how God values justice?

_____

_____

_____

_____

_____

Through Deborah, God beautifully displays His mercy to the Israelites even though they had again done evil in His eyes.

Review Judges 4:2–3, 6.

The mess Israel was in was massive, and they had a big part to play in it.

As a result of their running away from God, they ran right into the captivity of the king of Canaan, Jabin. Jabin's army commander was Sisera, whose claim to fame was using nine hundred chariots to cruelly oppress God's people for twenty years.

Little did Sisera know that God had a commander of His own: the warrior woman, Deborah.

One straight shooter, Deborah is a woman of God and she is assertive. We sometimes put Christian women under certain headers: quiet, timid, keeping to themselves. I don't see Deborah falling into any of these columns. Confident that what she has to say, she is saying for God, she "brings it."

Fulfilling her assignment as prophetess, Deborah delivers the word to Barak that God has given her. God is calling Barak to take ten thousand men to a designated spot where God will lure the enemy in and lead His people out to freedom.

Sometimes *God* says enough is enough. But other times He waits for us to say it first! That is the case here. The Israelites had agreed to obey God, even when Joshua asked them a second time in Joshua 24 if this is the way they wanted to go. Yet shortly after making this commitment, they knowingly turned from Him.

God loves His people. I can guarantee that if the Israelites would have surrendered their willful hearts that were against Him a long time ago, He would have come to their rescue. Yet, God honors the free will with which He created us. The love He wants from us is a love that is given freely to Him because we *want* to love Him. In this instance, it took Israel twenty years to get there. Sometimes we are a lot like the Israelites.

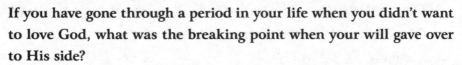

If you have gone through a period in your life when you didn't want to love God, what was the breaking point when your will gave over to His side?

Sitting down to share lunch together, tears streamed down my cheeks as Angie shared her own "before I loved God" story.

Before she even understood what it all meant, Angie's innocence was stolen. As a family friend took advantage of her childhood through abuse, shame made its home in her heart. Next, she was introduced to alcohol. Its numbing effect helped her hurting heart to forget, if only for a moment, the abuse that continued to come.

When alcohol no longer eased the pain, Angie found cocaine. When that wasn't enough, she found crack. The world of addiction suffocated her, yet fear of the unknown life outside her addiction kept her captive to its power. She would have months of sobriety, at least as those around her saw it, but as she shared with me, "Nothing changes when nothing changes." The arrests came again and again. One prison sentence. Two. It wasn't enough. Angie's addiction meant more to her than freedom.

Then, during her third incarceration, Angie reached the breaking point, what she calls "the gift of desperation." She used the word *gift* not in a biblical sense but because desperation helped her to surrender her life to Christ. She turned to God to find His love and a fresh start. Through the help of many surrounding her, she found her way to Jesus.

The new life God has given Angie is better. Easy? No. But oh-so-much better. That better comes often through the hands of other people.

Like Angie, Israel needed a fresh start; they needed help. Like Angie and Israel, we all need help; we all need God. Anything and everything else in life is secondary to our need for His forgiveness and salvation.

Deborah made her announcement to Barak. In essence: "God has heard the cries of His people, and He is sending help. That help is you."

Can you think of a time when you cried out to God for help and He sent a person?

_____

_____

_____

Is receiving help from people hard for you? If so, why?

_____

_____

_____

God's command to Barak was clear: Help God's people get free from the Canaanites. It also contained God's promise for Israel. He would go before them and lure the enemy into their hands.

According to Judges 4:6–7, how would you describe the manner in which Deborah delivered God's message to Barak?

_____

_____

Deborah sent for Barak and confidently brought God's word with no apologies. General Deborah told Barak exactly what God had said and there was no push-back from him. She obviously had behaved in such a way in her community that she held respect and authority, for that is what Barak gave her.

Calling on a person to step forward to help and defend others, Deborah didn't see this as a wimpy plea for help; this was Barak's assignment from God.

God created us, as humans and as the body of Christ, to need each other. This notion that it is weak to admit we need help and then ask for help is so far from God's best for us.

> *God created us*
> *to need each other.*

Galatians 6:2 shatters this myth concerning our independent ways: "By helping each other with your troubles, you truly obey the law of Christ" (NCV). Or as the NIV puts it, to "carry each other's burdens" is a mark that we are Christ's followers.

Please read Acts 4:32–35. What is one way that the early Christians helped each other?

_____

_____

When the believers were one in heart and mind, their automatic response was love. Sharing and helping each other wasn't a burden; they took care of one another because they loved one another.

In order to care for each other, we need to be in the know. *In what ways do those in my community need my help? In what way do I need help?*

Being a confident woman doesn't mean you are a woman who doesn't ask for help. Quite the opposite! A confident woman knows if she is going to be all God has called her to be, fulfilling the assignments God gives her, she's going to need other strong and skilled people helping her complete it. The assignment God brings your way will more than likely be above your natural ability. That is how God works so only He can receive the credit!

> *God calls us to appointments beyond our natural abilities so only He can receive the credit.*

So, friend, we have to get used to asking for and accepting help.

Let's review the definition of *confidence*: "full trust; belief in the powers, trustworthiness, or reliability of a person or thing."[18]

When we choose to believe in our community's ability and desire to come alongside us for help, we show confidence *in each other*. The best time to discover that your community is trustworthy and reliable is *before* you need them to be trustworthy and reliable. *Now* is when we need to show others we want to help them and then begin to allow others to help us as well.

Confidence doesn't mean we don't need each other; it means just the opposite. We recognize where our gifts and talents are limited and when we need help. The Israelites needed Deborah to lead them. Barak felt he needed Deborah to come alongside him. The confident woman above all else knows each and every day she is desperate for the help of Jesus. Just as Angie was. Just as you and I need to be.

Apply It

Did you grow up hearing, "God helps those who help themselves"? Maybe you were even led to believe that was a verse in the Bible.

How has the thinking that strength is displayed when you do it on your own impacted your ability to ask for help? How has it impacted your confidence?

_____

_____

_____

Take a few moments to create a list of how you need help.

_____

_____

_____

_____

Today, reach out to at least one person, expressing your need for his or her help in your life. If you are really feeling confident, go for two!

Finish up your time with the Lord today, asking Him to help you to have the courage to ask others for the help you need.

★

In This Together

MEMORY VERSE: "'So may all your enemies perish, LORD! But may all who love you be like the sun when it rises in its strength.' Then the land had peace forty years."—Judges 5:31

AS DEBORAH DELIVERED GOD'S DIRECTIONS, I imagine Barak rehearsed what he was up against: nine hundred chariots. For Israel's defense? There isn't a word that says Israel had even one! Imagine if our army was in this position: ten thousand men on foot versus nine hundred tanks. That would hardly be equitable.

That is exactly why this was God's plan—doing His work through His people in such a way that only He can get the glory!

Barak quickly asked for Deborah's help: "If you go with me, I will go; but if you don't go with me, I won't go" (Judges 4:8). Barak recognized the Spirit of God in Deborah and wanted her wisdom and strength with him.

At first glance, I was tempted to think Barak was weak. *You won't go fight unless you've got a woman with you?* Once I heard a sermon in which the pastor took the slant that Barak didn't have enough guts to go by himself. Yet I remember another Bible character, one who at first looked weak but became mighty through God. He also said similar words.

In Exodus 33:15, Moses said to God: "If your Presence does not go with us, do not send us up from here."

Though Solomon penned the words much later, Moses and Barak both knew the truth of Ecclesiastes 4:9: "Two are better than one, because they have a good return for their labor." That return was deliverance from their oppressors.

In Hebrews 11 we see these two commanders, Moses and Barak, in a grand list, numbered with others of great faith. Clearly, Barak's faith was not discounted because he and Deborah did the work together!

Digging Deeper

Reread Judges 4:6–10 for review if needed.

Barak and Deborah create a partnership to be used by God in a mighty way. To an outsider, God's command in verse 6—"Go, take with you ten thousand men" into battle—sounds terrifying. Yet, God followed His command with a promise: "I will lead Sisera, the commander of Jabin's army, with his chariots and his troops to the Kishon River and give him into your hands" (v. 7). God reassured Barak that as he said yes to God, God would take care of them. Barak would do his part and God would do His. And Deborah? Yes, she would be faithful to do her part as well.

And "Deborah also went up with him" (Judges 4:10).

Deborah came alongside Barak in the frightening task God had given him. She got in the trenches. She wasn't willing to call Barak to an action that she wasn't willing to do herself. And there, in the thick of battle, she continued to walk in confidence.

Deborah was a prophetess and a judge, not a commander or a soldier. "Warrior" was probably not listed in her top five strengths or in her gift mix. Yet when the tough time hit, Deborah was there. Deborah was God's spokesperson. This time she was bringing His encouragement to the battlefield and helping the commander of the army move.

Deborah's willingness to partner with God through Barak was not limited by her comfort level. Not only was Deborah obedient to deliver the message from God to Barak, she had no trouble getting right in the thick of things. She didn't call Barak out and then take her seat on the sidelines. She didn't just talk about obeying and doing big things for God. Deborah told Barak God was calling him to take ten thousand men and to head out against the enemy. And she went with him.

They were better together.

When I was raising my kids, I noticed a shift in television programming. I missed the subtleness of it as a teenager, but when I became a parent, I paid more attention to parental roles on TV.

Before I was born, TV shows depicted dads as kind, engaged, and leading their families. Growing up in the 1980s, that picture was shifting.

When Greg and I were raising our kids, I realized so many sitcoms were inappropriate for my family. I wasn't bothered that mothers were depicted as strong women. I wanted my daughters "to worry less about fitting into glass slippers and more about shattering glass ceilings."[19] But that is not what the TV trend was about. Men on comedies were treated as "less than." TV moms disrespected their TV husbands, with laughter of the recorded audience echoing in the background. The message seemed to be: If we put men down, women are lifted up.

That is not what I see in Deborah. She didn't take this opportunity to put a guy in his place. She didn't challenge Barak's manhood. She didn't need to. Deborah was confident in who she was. Deborah didn't pull Barak down a rung to lift herself up. She knew who and whose she was—God's.

I imagine her interactions with women would have been the same.

> *A confident woman doesn't have to pull another down to be lifted up.*

We have an obligation to love one another, to break the girl code for good. When it comes to cutting another down, competing with another woman for place or prestige, we have a command to do the opposite: Build her up. In the church, this harm can sometimes masquerade as "sharing" with another, bringing them "up to date," or even making a "prayer request," but our motives are not always pure. At least mine have not been.

Dissension and jealousy not only poison friendships but also our witness as God's children. God has more for us!

Here are five ways we can together break the girl code:

1. *Ask yourself.*

What if she read my mind? If she could hear my thoughts, would that be okay? Honestly, this one is enough to get me switching up my thoughts.

2. *Remind yourself.*

She is *not* my competition. We are both creations of God. There is enough of God for us both. His goodness, love, and power supply are unlimited.

> ## She is not the competition; she is God's creation.

3. *Pray.*

I find it nearly impossible to have negative feelings toward anyone when I pray God's best for her.

4. *Speak truth.*

I don't know all the details of her life, just as she does not know all the details of mine. Only God has the right to judge because He is perfect and has all the facts.

5. Desire change.

We may not be able to control thoughts that pop into our head, but we *can* control what we *do* with those thoughts. Ask the Lord to change your heart so your thoughts change. This is one prayer I know He is ecstatic to answer!

I have found that the more I ask God to change the way I think, the less frequently I have these unwanted thoughts.

When we are confident in who God has made us to be, we do not have to pull another down to be lifted up, be the person male or female. We can rest assured that in Christ, we are on our way to reaching our potential.

Apply It

If a particular person came to mind as you read the five steps for breaking the girl code, take a moment to confess this to God. Then express God's love to her (or him) via a handwritten note, text, email, or phone call.

Just as He had promised, God brings the victory to the Israelites in Judges 4. But wait! The enemy commander, Sisera, escapes!

At first glance, we could think God had slipped up. He promised He would "lead Sisera . . . and give him into [Barak's] hands." So why the escape move?

God is doing what God does best; setting the stage for His glory. He had said that the honor for this victory would not be Barak's; He would be handing Sisera over to a woman. In our next section, we'll meet this brave woman!

★

Common Tools for an Uncommon Purpose

MEMORY VERSE: "'So may all your enemies perish, Lᴏʀᴅ! But may all who love you be like the sun when it rises in its strength.' Then the land had peace forty years."—Judges 5:31

NOW'S THE TIME for us to go back and pick up the details we jumped over in Judges 4:11. This verse will provide an important piece to part two of our story: the entrance of our second heroine, Jael.

Digging Deeper

Please read Judges 4:11, 17–24.

Heber the Kenite, a descendant of Moses's brother-in-law, had separated himself from the rest of the Kenites. Now we see that God allowed this change to move his wife, Jael, into position.

Yes, God is again going to choose a woman for His work.

So often, we go about life thinking we are doing simple things. Making choices like going to school or joining the military, getting married or staying single, getting a job, finding a church family, buying a home, adopting a child. All the while, God is setting the stage for His next move. He is getting people and situations in place for a divine intersection at His appointed time.

Coincidences do not exist. Nor does fate. Calling divine appointments common engagements is cutting the Creator out of His glory.

> *Calling divine appointments common engagements is cutting the Creator out of His glory.*

Jael begins her assignment by inviting the enemy commander, Sisera, into her tent. Her home would become the location for her confident move. I highly doubt Jael would have had any forewarning that her dwelling would be needed for heavenly hospitality that day.

My friend Shelley told me about a time she had guests who were definitely "heavenly hospitality."

It was December, and not only was the hustle and bustle of Christmas upon her, but the third major surgery of the year for her oldest daughter was later that week. Shelley's church hosted a guest choir each year, a group of up to twenty-five children from Africa who, along with leaders and several chaperones, toured churches in the United States for six months of the year. She had known they were coming and knew that her family certainly had the room to provide a comfortable place to stay, but the busyness of life kept pushing the idea away.

Eventually Shelley offered the space her family had. As the time drew near, she felt tense and anxious with so much going on. They drove to the church to welcome the team and give them a ride home. Immediately she felt an overwhelming sense of joy and happiness that came from watching these children and chaperones. One of the children actually prayed for all of the host families as they were sent on their way, each with his or her temporary family. Shelley felt an immediate connection with the husband and wife team they were hosting. What could have been a stressful, untimely interruption in her family's schedule ended up being one of the most beautiful weekends! Shelley's family was able to provide a safe place for the couple to share their feelings and prayer requests. Using her home to do God's work was a blessing in disguise. This is what our Father asks of us: to give what we have. As *Jehovah-Jireh*, our provider, He is our source. He can take what we offer and multiply its impact.

Hebrews 13:2 tells us, "Do not forget to show hospitality to strangers, for by so doing some people have shown hospitality to angels without knowing it."

Working in her tent, Jael offered to God what she had; she showed hospitality to a stranger. While the commander of Jabin's army was no angel, God multiplied exponentially her gift!

Running away from his army, Sisera headed in the opposite direction as his army fled the battlefield. Commentaries say that being on foot, it would have taken him at least three days to arrive at the Kishon River.[20] Having just come from battle, he would have been weary and starving.

The man who had just days ago commanded an army of nine hundred chariots finds himself desperate for help in any form.

During this time period in history, men and women had separate tents. A woman's tent was considered a safe place, free of violence. Based on the tradition of nomadic people, once a stranger is admitted into your tent, he is safe. If Barak's soldiers were still chasing him, who would suspect that Sisera would be hidden in a woman's tent? This may be the reason Sisera felt secure when Jael offered her hospitality.

Picture Jael, covered from head to toe, perhaps her face as well, coming out to meet this man with the reputation of terrorizing nations. Her conversation reveals no fear, although I cannot imagine how hard her heart had to be beating! Leaning on her gifts of hospitality, she invites in the one who is on friendly terms with her community but is an enemy of God. Giving him the best of all she has, milk when he only asks for water, she offers him a place to sleep and even tucks him in. Talk about playing the part!

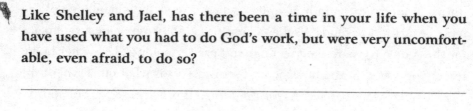

Like Shelley and Jael, has there been a time in your life when you have used what you had to do God's work, but were very uncomfortable, even afraid, to do so?

I cannot picture myself having the courage Jael displays as she then goes to Sisera while he sleeps, tent peg in one hand, hammer in the other, and sends him to his death.

A tent peg and a hammer would have been common tools for a wife of a nomad. Constantly on the move, taking down and putting up her tent would have been routine. How like God to use the routine work and the common tools of her everyday life to do His mighty work!

Commentator Matthew Henry describes Jael's heroism: "It was a divine power that enabled her to do it, and inspired her with a more than manly courage. What if her hand should shake, and she should miss her blow? What if he should awake when she was attempting it? Or suppose some of his own attendants should follow him, and surprise her in the face, how dearly would she and all hers be made to pay for it? Yet, obtaining the help of God, she did it effectually."[21]

Who is to say what could have prepared Jael for such a brave feat on that day? Had she more times than not found herself doing a "man's job"? Were her experiences similar to those of David the shepherd, when she had to protect herself from wild animals in the wilderness?

What experiences have you had in life that you would rather not have had but that prepared you for your future?

_____

_____

_____

_____

Whatever prior experience Jael may or may not have had, when she performed a job relegated to a man, God gave her the strength and courage to overcome any fear standing in her way. Nothing, not even having a terrorizing murderer in her home, held her back. That is the epitome of confidence!

On this day, God didn't use a strong soldier or a courageous commander to remove the enemy from power; He used a housewife, who was in fact a mighty warrior. A common woman doing everyday work took down the captain of nine hundred chariots!

God takes great pleasure in using everyday people to do extraordinary things! We see Him do so again and again in the Bible. Usually we would say that our God is not predictable. Yet using plain people is one of His most predictable plans!

> _Using plain people is one of God's most predictable plans._

Make a quick list of anyone you can think of in the Bible whom you would call "ordinary" but through whom God chose to work.

_____

_____

_____

Here are a few I came up with: Joseph, Moses, David, Esther, Mary the mother of Jesus, Peter. We could go on and on.

The last name I added to my list was me. I'm not in the Bible obviously, but honestly, you couldn't get any more "ordinary" than me. Growing up in a small Midwestern town, I was number seven of eight kids. I never got a degree. I got married young and started my family. I've spent the majority of my life as a work-at-home mom (including a stint as a homeschool teacher). Yes, God has assignments for us all!

Why do you think God doesn't stick to using only the highly educated, famous, or whatever culture considers to be "beautiful" people?

_____

_____

_____

The last few verses of our text answers this question clearly: "On that day God subdued Jabin the king of Canaan before the Israelites" (Judges 4:23).

Only God's name is listed as the victor. Not Jael, Barak, or Deborah. He is the plan maker, executer, and glory receiver. We get the privilege to participate in His great plan, but He gets all the glory!

Recall our memory verse from last week: "Now faith is confidence in what we hope for and assurance about what we do not see" (Hebrews 11:1).

Faith—that is what these women and Barak possessed. They put their confidence in God and in His promise. When God said He would go before them and make sure they had the victory, they had confidence that He would do what He said He would do. They trusted, they believed, and they relied on God. Though they could not see the conclusion, they believed in God's guarantee.

If you have time today, maybe on a lunch break or before you head to bed, I encourage you to read all of Hebrews 11. (It took me less than five minutes.) Talk about a faith builder! After reading of the relentless belief of these God followers, my faith was bolstered.

But when I did read Hebrews 11, I couldn't help but notice one discrepancy.

In Hebrews 11:32, whose name from our story is listed?

_____

_____

What playmakers are left out of the list?

_____

_____

As you realize this omission, does it make you feel any certain way?

_____

_____

Of course, Deborah and Jael never read the New Testament to realize they were left out, but I really think they would be okay with it. The confident woman doesn't *need* the spotlight. Our craving for other people's approval lessens because we know that we already have approval—God's. The women obeyed God. They completed His assignment. They didn't have to have an "atta-girl" from anyone but Him.

> *A confident woman doesn't crave
> other people's approval because
> she already has God's.*

I'd love to say, "Me too!" So self-assured, I don't need reassurance from another. I'm not quite there yet, but learning about the faith of these amazing women is moving me closer!

When you have served well, made a hard choice, or gone above and beyond, what is the reaction of your heart if no one notices?

_____

_____

Maybe you're wondering why I know Deborah would have been okay with being left out of the Hall of Fame. You're about to find out in our next section.

From Jael today we see: God truly sets up divine appointments. With the confidence He provides, we can recognize these divine appointments, acknowledging that they are not common engagements but an opportunity to give glory to our God. While we may think we are simply doing life, God is in fact preparing us for His purpose, just as He did Deborah and Jael. And when He does, in His strength, we will have the confidence and courage to step right past fear and participate in His plan!

Apply It

God used a tent peg and a hammer in the hands of Jael to fulfill His divine purpose. As a woman in a nomadic tribe, these were everyday items. Yet Jael used them in a very uncommon way to accomplish her assignment.

What are some of the common "tools" of your everyday life?

_____

_____

Mine include a computer, paper and pens, my Bible and commentaries, all of my kitchen appliances, my car, and my washer and dryer.

How could you use the tools of your everyday work to confidently serve God?

_____

_____

Let's ask God today to reveal to us how our common tools can be used for His uncommon purposes and in this way fulfill His purpose for our lives.

Come back to this space later and share what tools you used and how you were able to use them to give God glory.

★

Like the Sun

MEMORY VERSE: "'So may all your enemies perish, Lᴏʀᴅ! But may all who love you be like the sun when it rises in its strength.' Then the land had peace forty years."—Judges 5:31

SO I LEFT YOU HANGING a bit in our last section. You want to know how we can know Deborah was okay not being in the spotlight?

Let's pick up the end of Deborah's story in the passage my Bible calls, "The Song of Deborah."

Digging Deeper

Please read Judges 5:1–5.

In these verses, to whom does Deborah give credit?

_____

_____

In this song written by Deborah and Barak, Deborah shouts, "Sing it again!" as she gives God all the glory. Together they sing of God's faithfulness: He did exactly what He said He would do!

Following their successful day, there would surely have been opportunity for Deborah to get a pat on the back or a fist bump.

Yet she uses her influence to point the praise right back to God. She challenges others, no matter their position in life, to do the same!

Read Judges 5:10–11. Who does Deborah address first?

_____

_____

In verse 10 as translated in the NIV, *recite* means "to give, place, add, send forth."[22] It's used with regard to something given, whether tangible or intangible.

According to this definition, what is being given in Judges 5:10–11?

_____

_____

_____

It saddens me to think of how often God answers a prayer or does exactly what I needed Him to do, but I forget to recite His victory. Sometimes the first person to whom I tell my good news is my husband or a friend. By the time I share with them, life often swings right back into busy and I bypass giving praises to the Lord.

Here, Deborah uses her influence and leadership in a responsible way. Not with manipulation, but in calling out to others to do what is right.

As she progresses through her story, she includes a bit about herself. Earlier, Deborah was given the title prophetess and we know she is a judge.

What is the title Deborah gives herself in Judges 5:7?

_____

What are the characteristics of a mother that would apply to Deborah in her role with Israel?

_____

_____

How would this role to Israel contrast to her roles as judge and prophetess?

_____

_____

When I looked up the definition of the word translated *mother* from the original Hebrew, the first few words were the ones I expected: "mother" or "grandmother." I didn't expect "fork," as in fork in the road.[23]

Strange, but isn't that exactly what Deborah was? In her additional role of mother in Israel, she created a fork in the road. A place where Barak and Israel would choose no longer to go against the Lord or continue their journey away from God. Thankfully, they made that wise choice and it led to peace in their land for forty years (Judges 5:31).

Like a true mother, Deborah "calls out" her children in verse 8 (ESV): "When new gods were chosen, then war was in the gates. Was shield or spear to be seen among forty thousand in Israel?" She basically tells them: "You chose new gods; other things had your heart. Yet when trouble came to our country, you were nowhere to be found."

As she continues, Deborah doesn't judge the people harshly. It would have been so easy to say, "Twenty years of oppression? You were just getting what you deserve for turning from the Lord!"

Instead, even as she reprimands them, Deborah doesn't hold their sin against them. "My heart goes out to the commanders of Israel who offered themselves willingly among the people. Bless the LORD" (v. 9 ESV).

I really thought I had it all together as a young girl. Constantly paying more attention to others' lives rather than my own, the plank sticking out of my own eye was obnoxious. I know my hypocritical heart tripped up more than one person, causing them to not want a relationship with Jesus if *that* was what it looked like. As I grew older, in His merciful way, God kindly opened my eyes to the depth of my pride. I was humiliated at what I saw lurking there. And yet, as ugly as it was, on my own, I simply did not possess the power to rid myself of it. What began with counseling when I was eighteen years old has led to a lifetime of depending on the Lord to show me what I cannot see and to take away this despicable sin of self-righteousness.

It has only been in the past couple of years that I have come to the realization that the pathway that led to all the blessings I have experienced in life has not been simply because I made wise choices and good decisions. No, the truth is I was a young girl who hadn't experienced that much pain or trouble in life . . . yet.

Let's continue to observe the confidence of Deborah displayed.

Read Judges 5:15–18.

What might Deborah mean when she says in verse 15, "In the districts of Reuben there was much searching of heart"?

_____

_____

Deborah goes on to ask some hard-hitting questions of some of the tribes. Basically, *why did you stay preoccupied with your day-to-day busyness when God had something for His people to do?* Again, you don't see Deborah struggling with people pleasing. Her confidence is built on God's approval, not people approval, so she can say the hard things.

> *When confidence is built on God's approval, not people approval, we can say the hard things.*

Her song goes on, past verse 18, and then, in the middle of her detailed description of the battle, one sentence stands out. Spot it for yourself.

Read Judges 5:21–22. What line is slipped in and sandwiched between the description of the river Kishon sweeping away the enemy and the thundering of the warhorses? See it?

_____

_____

So odd and yet so very beautiful!

The word here that is translated *soul* means "to breathe, be refreshed." It is the Hebrew concept of *nepes*, meaning the inner self versus the outer appearance. "The term is often used in phrases which relate either to the loss of life or its preservation and sustenance."[24]

What glimpse might this phrase give us into Deborah's heart?

_____

_____

Can I just tell you how much I love this short sentence? These six words, *March on, my soul, with might!* (ESV), tell me Deborah was a woman who needed a bit of self-talk, and she knew just when and how to bring it.

Maybe just thinking of all that was at stake and all that had transpired that day, she was worn out, battle weary. Could it be that after such intense interactions she felt weary, like her days of leading Israel could be done?

I have to admit, I'm feeling that way right now. It's been a long, hard week at the Cowell house . . . and it's only Tuesday! Everything in me wants to crawl onto my couch and say, "Done!" I don't want any more, especially not this week. Over it!

I've got to do exactly what Deborah has done! "March on, Lynn! Be strong!" I've got to say to myself, "You go, girl! Keep going!" How about you?

This year, a door opened in my work that, while wonderful and exciting, would be way over my head to accomplish. Without even a single prayer, I headed to my office to write an email simply saying no.

Then I stopped.

What if this was God? Could it be? Would God ask me to do something that was beyond my normal strength?

Yes, that did sound like it could in fact be a plan He would create. He *would* plan to put me in a place beyond my ability. I stopped and instead of heading to my computer I went to the chair where I begin each day with the Lord. I opened my scheduled passage for that day and read:

> *"May the God of endurance and encouragement grant you to live in such harmony with one another, in accord with Christ Jesus."*—Romans 15:5 (esv)

I was stunned! I have read my Bible many times through and the book of Romans more times than that and I do not believe I have *ever seen* God called the God of endurance and encouragement. God knew! He knew that if I was going to say yes to this assignment and have the courage to take it on, I was going to have to know that He is in fact the God of endurance!

Deborah understood that we must encourage ourselves. There will not always be friends and family surrounding us, telling us to keep going. But there is the Holy Spirit, residing in us, giving us the help we need.

There are many days I have to whisper under my breath like Deborah, "Keep going, Lynn! Keep going!" Your heart needs that self-cheering too!

Deborah preaches again to herself in Judges 5:12 (esv), "Awake, awake Deborah! Awake, awake, break out in a song!"

She finishes her song revealing the source of her incredible strength: "So may all your enemies perish, Lord! But may all who love you be like the sun when it rises in its strength" (Judges 5:31). Our memory verse for this chapter.

To what does the psalmist compare God in Psalm 84:11?

_____

_____

Deborah says, "May all who love you be like the sun when it rises in its strength." We are compared to the sun. Then in the Psalms, David compares God to the sun. And so it should be, for we are created in God's image (Genesis 1:27).

Deborah's strength came from her love for the Lord. Her love for Him empowered her to be like the sun as it comes up morning after morning, consistent and powerful.

This truth is the foundation on which we can build a confidence that is deeply rooted, that never slips or fades, that's unshakable. As Paul so profoundly said, "So that Christ may dwell in your hearts through faith—that you, being rooted and grounded in love, may have strength to comprehend with all the saints what is the breadth and length and height and depth, and to know the love of Christ that surpasses knowledge, that you may be filled with all the fullness of God" (Ephesians 3:17–19 ESV). When we understand, in the deepest places of our soul and being, how grandly the Father loves us, it changes us in a way that can never be taken from us!

When we understand that He is wild for us (Psalm 45:11 MSG), a confidence takes hold that is sure, stable, and secure. It is a trust that, no matter what comes to crush and defeat us, His foundation of love stands firm.

We'll finish our time today in 1 John 4:16–18.

The two words _rely on_ used in 1 John 4:16 are _pisteuo_ in the Greek: "to believe, put one's faith in, trust."[25] We may not have been able to believe or put faith in the love of a human on earth. We may have been disappointed, hurt, ruined in our own eyes. Others have failed us and we have failed them. Yet this love, God's perfect, unconditional, never-ending love, is the one love we can have confidence in. This trust allows us to have faith in God when we can't have faith in others. When trust has been broken or circumstances seem beyond repair, we know the love God has for us. We recognize, understand, and rely on His love.

Based on 1 John 4:16–18, why can we trust this love?

_____

_____

God is love. Love is not simply what He says He will give us; love is who He is. You and I are made perfect—finished, fulfilled, and completed—in this love.

Apply It

Friend, would you soak in the power of these words of Truth? You and I, no matter our situation today, confident or not confident, walking in the fullness of God or struggling every day to believe, have our God at work in us. Every day He is casting out fear with His love. Each morning He is pouring out His perfect love on you and opening a way for you to be free from all fear and doubt.

Today, repeat to yourself over and over and over again this heart-changing truth: *Perfect love casts out all fear. Perfect love casts out all fear.* His perfect love—for me, toward me, in me, and through me—is casting out all fear from me.

Here, in His perfect love, I find my confidence, and together we can do anything!

Group Discussion Questions

Read this week's memory verse aloud, as a group or select an individual to do so: "'So may all your enemies perish, LORD! But may all who love you be like the sun when it rises in its strength.' Then the land had peace forty years."—Judges 5:31

1. In Judges 4, we meet Deborah living out her familiar calling as judge and then, without hesitation, going into battle. What part could past obedience to God have played in preparing Deborah for this role where confidence was now required?

2. Read Judges 4:2–3, 6. Lynn said, "Tough environments for our assignments can condition us to build our confidence on Christ alone." Why does God time and time again set His people up in situations that are physically beyond what they are capable of?

3. In what tough environments do you find yourself that push the limits of your current level of confidence? How might this be God at work?

4. Today's memory verse is Deborah's prayer that we would be as strong as the sun. What traits describe the sun that can help us when confidence is required?

5. Dependent on the power of the Holy Spirit, what is one practical step you can take this week in your tough environment?

6. Wrap up your time together this week praying for one another and the situations you face that *demand* that you have Christ's confidence. Share with one another Scriptures that come to mind and write them down to refer to during the week.

Abigail & Michal

WHEN CONFIDENCE IN RELATIONSHIPS IS QUESTIONED

★

PRAYER: *Lord, so often in life I find myself in situations completely out of my control. Many times, this is due to someone else's actions. Help me to learn, Father, that when my confidence is built on You, my courage remains—even if circumstances are outside of my control. My security is in You. In Jesus' name, Amen.*

MEMORY VERSE: "God is within her, she will not fall; God will help her at break of day."—Psalm 46:5

Meet Michal

SITTING IN THE STANDS SURROUNDED BY THOUSANDS, I was enjoying being with people I love. Splurging for a special treat, my husband had purchased tickets to a professional basketball game for our entire family. (Yes, that is a treat for me. I really like sports.) I made sure to sit by the louder people in my family so I could do a lot of yelling and laughing. The evening was just what I had hoped it would be . . . until that time. You know *that time* when all the showgirls come out, the ones who have all the curves in all the right places?

Yep, halftime.

As I sat watching the performance, I caught myself thinking, *How do they look like that?* After a few moments, I began to pay attention to my thoughts and silently countered, *What are you doing? Why are you thinking that? Those girls are half your age!* I got myself together and changed the thoughts I was filling my heart with.

I chose to change what I was thinking that evening because I don't want to examine myself through the lens of the illusion that we *can* all be the same. We are each created differently, with different gifts, talents, abilities, *and* bodies.

The woman I want to be is the one so comfortable with who I am that I don't worry about who others are. And what I really want is to be so confident in who I am that I help others become confident in who they are.

To be *that* woman, I need to be loving, joyful, peaceful, and patient. My heart needs to be so full of God's goodness that when I walk in a room full of strangers, I don't worry about what others think of me or if I'll fit in. My purpose is to make others feel important, cared for, and loved.

But I'm not always that woman. In fact, sometimes, when I am not feeling confident at all, I make it all about me. *What will they think of me? Will my outfit fit in? Will my hair be okay? Will they like me? Who will I talk to and what will I talk about?*

I know; it's pitiful.

Have you ever found yourself stuffing your mind with thoughts similar to mine? Chances are you were not at a sporting event. You might have been watching one though! Or you could have been shopping, gazing in a display window, when you thought, *If I could just fit into those jeans!* Soaking in a romantic movie, you watch the lovely actress and wish, *If only I didn't have these wrinkles or rolls!* Scrolling through your Instagram, you wish for a wardrobe like hers. Yep, I've been there too! And as our thoughts go downhill, our confidence goes with it.

This week our study is the tale of two princesses of sorts. When I say princesses, you might think pink and tulle and crowns and stuff like that. These gals weren't those kinds of princesses. In fact, these two were around well before tulle.

We'll start with Michal. In 1 Samuel 14:49 we are first introduced to this daughter of Saul, King of Israel. You have to feel a bit sorry for this girl from the very start.

You know how engagement proposals can be very staged nowadays? Set up just right for a social media moment? Michal had none of that glitter or glory! King Saul, her dad, played "Let's Make a Deal" with David, formerly known as Shepherd Boy. Ever since that killing-a-giant thing, the whole country was crazy about David. Hero-status-parades-in-the-streets kind of thing. And Saul couldn't take it.

Digging Deeper

<u>Read 1 Samuel 18:6–16.</u> **Name at least two sources for King Saul's jealousy of David.**

_____

_____

Can you think of a time when you have struggled with jealousy or envy? What was the source of that jealousy?

_____

_____

_____

I hate to admit it, but the jealousy I have wrestled with is all too similar to Saul's. Seeing God have favor on or use other people, my mind has wandered to the ugly: *Why them? Why not me?* I fail to see all God has done for me and in me. Self-pity has found a comfortable residence in a heart that has so very much to be thankful for.

King Saul didn't just let his mind go to the wrong place, though. To rid himself of this nemesis David, King Saul came up with a scheme. First Samuel 18:20–27 goes on to tell of Saul's proposition to David: If David would kill a hundred Philistines, he would be rewarded with Michal, Saul's daughter, in marriage. King Saul never planned to attend a wedding. He believed his proposal would end at a funeral. David would be killed trying to accomplish this feat. And. Then. It. Would. Be. Over. David dead. Jealousy gone. King Saul could go on happily ever after.

Saul forgot one element in his equation: The Lord was on David's side. "In everything he did he had great success, because the LORD was with him" (1 Samuel 18:14). David not only killed one hundred Philistines, he killed two hundred! Instead of David being killed in battle, a few chapters later in 1 Samuel 31, King Saul is the one critically wounded in a war and ends up taking his own life.

David is now king.

That's about as fairy-tale as this story gets. What happens next between David and Michal is where our focus will be. Michal's story makes me think this gal learned a bit or two from her daddy about how to treat other people.

As king, David plans a homecoming of sorts in the capital city; he is bringing the ark of God to Jerusalem. Once held captive by the Philistines, it's time to celebrate as the ark moves from Baale-judah to its rightful resting place in the city of David.

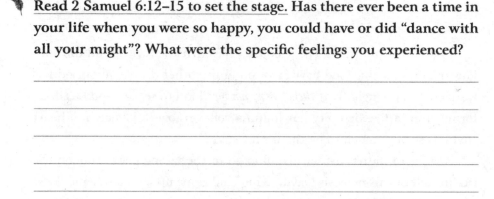

Read 2 Samuel 6:12–15 to set the stage. Has there ever been a time in your life when you were so happy, you could have or did "dance with all your might"? What were the specific feelings you experienced?

_____

_____

_____

_____

During this David dance, he was wearing a linen ephod, which was a piece of clothing that those who served God wore under another piece of clothing. In this case, the linen ephod would have been under David's kingly robe. Partying in the streets, David ditched his robe so he could dance even better!

Now this dance is more than just grooving a little. The word here used for dancing meant he was springing round in half circles to the sound of music; resting on the heel of the left foot as he spun.[26]

While all this celebrating is going on, where is Michal, his wife? Right next to him? Rejoicing and dancing with her king?

Second Samuel 6:16 reveals where Michal was. Write the word that describes her feelings toward her husband during this dance.

_____

_____

Michal is *looking down* on David, both literally and figuratively. She is not happy with David being so happy. Second Samuel 6:16 says, "And when she saw King David leaping and dancing before the LORD, she despised him in her heart."

Despised. Now there's an ugly word. It means "to regard with disgust or disdain."[27] Michal looked down on David for how he chose to celebrate and worship God. She obviously felt his sheer joy in bringing the ark to the City of David was inappropriate and embarrassing to her.

So, she despised him in her heart.

Say out loud "in her heart." Remember that phrase. It's going to be very important during this chapter.

This ugly distaste for David festered, rotting in her heart.

As our story progresses, 2 Samuel 6:20, says, "David returned home to bless his household." He is so excited about this amazing day he's had honoring and giving praise to God! He's walking toward the door, with "Honey, I'm home" on his lips. Michal comes out to meet him.

Remember what the Bible said Michal felt toward David? Lovey-dovey? Warm and fuzzy? Not hardly.

Again, write the word that spoke of Michal's feelings toward David.

_____

_____

Michal had no regard for how the Lord would have looked upon David's heart of worship. Consumed with her own humiliation, her mind couldn't get past what her eyes had seen.

As David enters, Michal's sarcasm-laced words spew out all over him. "How the king of Israel has distinguished himself today, going around half-naked in full view of the slave girls of his servants as any vulgar fellow would!" (2 Samuel 6:20).

"Disrobing" or "half-naked" in the Hebrew means "uncovered, exposed, naked."[28]

One thing we tend to do when we feel humiliated, angry, fearful, embarrassed, or intimidated is exaggerate. *You do that every time! Why do you always . . .?*

Why do you think that we sometimes over-exaggerate?

Was David really half-naked? No, Michal inflated the situation. What was really exposed and uncovered was Michal's heart. She allowed the feelings *in her heart* to flow *out of her mouth*, just as Matthew 12:34 says.

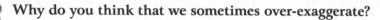

Feelings filling our heart eventually flow out of our mouth.

Michal was making this about her. Not about glorifying God or even focusing on David. It was all about Michal.

From here, Michal and her marriage went downhill.

When we are in potentially embarrassing situations, our insecurities are stirred up, and our confidence can slip. They don't have to! We can learn to lean into the power of the Holy Spirit to come and comfort us and give us His wisdom and strength so we can respond with confidence.

We can overcome this self-deception by honestly asking ourselves what and why. *What* am I feeling? *Why* am I feeling this way?

Michal could have taken a few moments to analyze her own heart before David arrived home. She could have gone to a quiet place, removed herself, until she had a chance to process what was going on inside of her. She could have asked God to help her with the feelings that were trying to control her.

For a moment, pretend *you* are Michal. Write the answer to these questions:

What **am I feeling?**

_____

_____

Why **am I feeling this way?**

_____

_____

Was it fear of what others would think? Proverbs 29:25 (ESV) tells us, "The fear of man lays a snare, but whoever trusts in the LORD is safe." Michal was definitely caught in a snare, a trap of rashness and irritation. With God's help, she could have had victory over her fear of what others would think of her and her parading husband.

Was it pride? If so, she could have recognized her elevated sense of self-importance and saved herself from a fall.

Slowing down and testing her heart and mind could have saved Michal from the actions she would one day regret, but Michal neither slowed down nor tested her heart. She allowed her lack of confidence to determine her actions, resulting in painful consequences in her future.

One of the wisest things you and I can do is learn from other people, especially from their mistakes.

Michal didn't do what she could have done. She allowed her doubt to determine how she reacted to a difficult situation. She could have turned to the Lord for the courage she needed to remain calm.

Apply It

You and I *can* make that choice. When our feelings try to force us forward, we *can*, through the power of the Holy Spirit, **stop**. We may not be strong enough to stop the swirling in our own strength, but we can stop our reactions with the Spirit's power. We can *always* stop long enough to pray this single-word prayer: *Help.*

Today, let's practice our single word prayer.

Lord, help. In Jesus' name, Amen.

★

Wisdom We Need When We Need It

MEMORY VERSE: "God is within her, she will not fall; God will help her at break of day."—Psalm 46:5

LET'S STEP BACK A FEW CHAPTERS to 1 Samuel 23. Israel is in a season of unrest because her leader, King Saul, is in a state of unrest. Instead of focusing on leading God's people, he is fueled by jealous rage at David (23:15). He has left his throne and "come out to take" David's life. This situation in the desert might not have been blasted on social media, but word of Saul's behavior against Israel's hero spread. All of Israel would have had to pick sides.

David or Saul?

In the middle of this chase, traipsing across the Israeli country-side, Samuel dies. Samuel, the prophet and Israel's last judge, God's voice to God's people and the glue of the nation, is gone.

Just as you and I are aware when our world is in unrest, Abigail, the heroine of our story, would have heard the news: Samuel is dead. "All Israel assembled and mourned for him" (1 Samuel 25:1). Being the wise woman she was, Abigail would have been sensitive to how this might impact her world.

Four hours from home and from the place she felt safest, my daughter texted me from college: *Did you see there was another bombing?*

Another bombing in a string of terrorism. Attending a large university, her weekly activities often involved large gatherings of people. Exactly the type of venues the recent terrorist attacks targeted. She was scared for good reason.

All three of my children were attending major universities at the time. The unrest in the world was doing everything it could to stir up the unrest in my mama heart.

What goes through a woman's mind when her world is in crisis? All too often it soaks in thoughts of worry until saturated with crippling fear.

But we have a choice. We can choose to step back from the crazy and close our eyes. We can breathe in God's majesty and greatness and focus on His faithfulness.

We can also choose to stay in the whirlwind of worry.

What we choose and where we go in our mind will have consequences.

Should I praise God for His faithfulness in my past, my heart will be propelled to trust again. His presence will come into my situation and comfort me. King David himself sang, "Yet you are holy, enthroned on the praises of Israel" (Psalm 22:3 ESV). When we sing His praises, we are reminded of His rightful place in our lives: on the throne.

Praising God for His faithfulness in my past propels my heart to trust again.

Digging Deeper

Read 1 Samuel 25:1–3.

Here we are introduced to two additional characters. We've met David. We'll add a fellow named Nabal and his wife, Abigail. Abigail is described as "intelligent and beautiful" (v. 3). The Hebrew word here for *intelligent* means "good."[29] We will see from her story she was also very wise. Not a one-time-I-got-it-right kind of wisdom either. Wise was whom she was. Where did this kind of wisdom come from?

Psalm 51:6 says, "Yet you desired faithfulness even in the womb; you taught me wisdom in that secret place."

Every day, we saturate our minds in our media of choice. It might appear we believe wisdom comes from the newest podcast or the latest news update.

The New King James Version states Psalm 51:6 this way, "Behold, You desire truth in the inward parts, and in the hidden part You will make me to know wisdom." And in the ESV, it says God's wisdom is taught in the "secret heart."

God desires for us to experience His truth, His firmness, and His faithfulness—the picture of confidence. He wants us to experience this stability in our innermost being, in the hidden place, the deepest part of our heart. He wants His confidence to reside in that place no one else sees. There He will make known to us wisdom; there He can show us our next move. *Known* in this verse is the Hebrew word *yada*. Some of its many definitions include: "clearly understand, instruct, know for certain, to make known and intimately."[30] In the deepest part of my heart, the intimate places that only He knows, there He will give me His wisdom.

I need this deep kind of wisdom. Wisdom that comes from the depths of God's heart to the deepest part of mine. When I am upset, unglued, or uncertain, I need a wisdom only God can provide. When my world is shaken by rocky relationships or failing finances, I need a confident wisdom that knows, on Christ my solid rock, all will be well.

> *I need a wisdom that comes from the depths of God's heart to the deepest part of mine.*

That is the kind of confidence Abigail will need in her very near future.

As we read her description—"discerning and beautiful" (ESV)—from most women's perspective, Abigail has it all! On top of that, her husband is wealthy. Many of us would think, *What more is there?*

As Lysa TerKeurst says though: "Her life is a package deal. You get the good and the bad."[31] This is so true of Abigail! Often when a sentence is written, the good comes first, but watch out for what comes after the "but."

"She was smart and beautiful, but [her husband] was mean-spirited and bad-tempered, *an embarrassment to* his Calebite tribe" (1 Samuel 25:3b The Voice).

Mean-spirited and bad-tempered—it just doesn't get much worse for husband material. In the Hebrew, the word *mean-spirited* is *qaseh*, meaning "to be tough, hardened, hard servitude, severe, harsh words, inflexible, stubborn."[32] This word sprang from the Israelites' agricultural life, a picture of a heavy yoke put on oxen to force them to do what they did not want to do. Since these yokes were extremely heavy, the oxen would resist. Nabal, whose very name meant "fool," resisted God's Spirit in his life, which was so counter to the reputation of his tribal ancestor Caleb.

 Drawing from our teaching in Week 3 on Rahab, how are Nabal and Caleb different?

Nabal . . . such a contrast to his wife, whose very name means "cause of joy."

Read 1 Samuel 25:4–44 for their entire story.

While David was running for his life from Saul, six hundred men had gathered around him. That is some crowd to have to manage! They had chosen the Desert of Maon as their camp, where according to verse 7, it was sheep-shearing time.

For ancient Hebrews and eastern cultures, sheep were an integral part of their daily sustenance—for food, clothing, and offerings. Sheep-shearing was an important season as sheep were a chief part of their financial portfolio. Shearing meant payday!

Let's take a look at how our three characters each behave in this tenuous situation and what impact their actions bring.

David approaches Nabal, via his servants, in 1 Samuel 25.6. Humbly, he asks Nabal for provisions for his men. His crew had been providing protection to Nabal's shepherds from wild beasts or possibly wandering Arabs, who believed they had a right to take whatever they came upon, including these valuable tender creatures.

David's request for food from Nabal isn't over the top. Nabal had three thousand sheep and one thousand goats. One sheep will feed approximately forty adults. If David had asked for enough meat to feed his men, it would have equaled .005 percent of Nabal's net worth. Hardly enough to get ugly about when David's men had provided protection for Nabal's flocks.

What are some words you would use to describe Nabal's answer to David in verses 10–11?

_____

_____

Nabal shows just how much of a simpleton he is. With cocky words, he lives up to his name.

How would you describe David's reaction to Nabal's answer in verse 13?

_____

_____

Then there is Abigail. When the servant came to give her the report of all that had taken place between these two, she also had an opportunity to react.

Abigail could have chosen fear. There was a lot to be afraid of! First Samuel 22:2 describes what type of men were in David's "troop": "And everyone who was in distress, and everyone who was in debt, and everyone who was bitter in soul, gathered to him. And he became commander over them. And there were with him about four hundred men" (ESV). Angry, hungry vagabonds were en route to her home!

Scripture tells us: "Abigail wasted no time" (25:18 NLT). In Hebrew, this phrase means "to be quick, hasten, hurry, do at once."[33] It can also mean "disturbed," which I am sure she was. Upon hearing this fearful news, she moved quickly into gear. But she didn't just react on her emotions. She lost no time in putting together a wise plan that entailed personally going out to the desert to speak to David.

I wonder if Abigail's personality type caused her to naturally be bold and brave? We don't know; we're only told she was "intelligent and beautiful." Outward beauty wasn't going to save her family at this point though; she would need much more.

Since Abigail didn't delay, would you agree it is safe to say she wasn't scared?

The time had finally come to host our family reunion, and Greg and I were determined to show our extended family the best time. Renting a home in the mountains, we picked a location close to a natural water slide known as Slippery Rock. Research told us there were steps leading to the top, a rope to hold on to, and a lifeguard at the bottom.

The evening before our outing, the keeper of the cabin stopped by to offer any help we might need. Informing her of our plans, she quickly pointed us in another direction. Slippery Rock was so crowded and a bit of a drive, she said. Why not go to a waterfall that was even more fun, close by, and that hardly anyone knew about? Jotting down her directions, we appreciated the input from a local.

The next day the twelve of us piled into our cars, heading into the national forest. Finding the waterfall just where she had said, we unloaded our towels and got our cameras ready to record the fun.

My son went first, being the daring one. Mariah, our middle, soon followed. Once our little one approached the top, Greg and I began to feel uncomfortable. "Wait up, honey! Let Daddy go with you!" I instructed Madi. Soon Greg reached the top and plopped our tiny girl onto his lap. They were off. No sooner had Greg pushed off from the ledge than his face changed. Something was wrong, terribly wrong. The water was not pushing them down the middle, as it had the rest of our family. Madi and Greg were heading straight for the solid stone wall. Greg quickly reacted, sticking out his leg. No longer would their heads hit the granite; his back would. Unaware of exactly what was happening from down below, I tried to discern what was taking place. I only knew that everything was not alright.

When Greg and Madi reached the bottom, Greg's grimace revealed his pain. Requesting a towel, he asked his father to check his back. The next thing I knew, Greg, our son Zach, and Grandpa Duge were piling into the car to find an emergency room for stitches.

Greg's quick reaction, using his leg as a break for their bodies, could very well have saved their lives that day. He had confidently made a tough decision on the spot. His wisdom for sure saved the day, but just because he was quick on his feet didn't mean he wasn't scared.

Has there been a time in your life when you have felt your situation was out of control and you had to react quickly? What wisdom did you rely on to make that decision?

_____

_____

_____

Being brave isn't the absence of fear; it is making your move in the presence of it.

> *Being brave isn't the absence of fear; it is making your move in the presence of it.*

Apply It

Is there a decision in your life you need to make? End your study time today by boldly asking God to give you the wisdom you need to respond to the situations in your life confidently. Trust that not only will He provide the wisdom you need but the peace to go with it.

★

Doing a Man's Job

MEMORY VERSE: "God is within her, she will not fall; God will help her at break of day."—Psalm 46:5

IN OUR STUDY, we have seen several women who knew the moves they needed to make, even if those moves were normally reserved for men only.

Joan of Arc was born in France in 1412, the daughter of a peasant trained by her mother to sew and spin, definitely not for the life of a soldier. Yet at age twelve, Joan began to hear a voice. She believed this voice was God, instructing her to be brave and bold and play a part in setting her country free from the tyranny of England. Her family would never allow her to do what only men could do. Knowing she had to obey God, Joan left all she had ever known to do so. As she put it: "Since God commanded it, had I had a hundred fathers and a hundred mothers, had I been born a king's daughter, I should have departed."[34]

Joan, finding an unshakable confidence in the God who had called her, boldly approached those who ruled locally. Using a wisdom beyond her years and training, she convinced them to give her an army. Joan went into battle with four thousand men, a suit of armor created specifically for her, and a banner reading, "Of the Party of the King of Heaven."

Joan believed that she was not limited by her sex, her size, or the strife around her leadership. She trusted God was with her and working through her, and she experienced victory on the battlefield.

This young girl went against all odds to do what she felt God had compelled her to do. But not everyone believed in Joan or the unique relationship she claimed to have with God. On May 30, 1431, Joan was burned at the stake for hearing voices and wearing men's clothing. Even while she paid the ultimate price for making her move with God, Joan repeatedly called out, "Jesus!"

My mind cannot wrap itself around the fear Joan would have encountered over and over again.

Going before the government. Leading thousands of men into battle. Being burned at the stake.

Where did she get a courage and a confidence like that?

History tells us Joan's mother had taught her at a very young age to pray, to spend her days communing with God.

We would be wise women if we chose to spend our days communing with God as well. For each of us, this may look a bit different. You may choose to pray in the morning and then set an alarm to stop and take a break to pray again later in the day. I enjoy and find the need to talk to God all day long. In front of my mirror putting on my makeup, bending over the ironing board, driving my car, and in sudsy dishwater up to my elbows . . . these places are all "altars" for me—places where I talk to God. The more I talk to Him throughout the day, the more aware I am of His presence continually with me, giving me the direction and wisdom I need . . . sometimes minute by minute.

By pouring God's truth into our minds and hearts, we are prepared when trouble and turmoil hit our lives. Jesus tells us, "I have told you these things, so that in me you may have peace. In this world you *will* have trouble. But take heart! I have overcome the world" (John 16:33, emphasis mine). Jesus makes it clear, trouble is part of living on this planet. He also says in Him we can have the peace we need when that time comes.

According to 1 Samuel 25:18, who is Abigail's back-up for her mission?

_____

_____

While having a team is ideal, it appears Abigail didn't have a pile of girlfriends backing her up or a team of coworkers preparing this huge undertaking. I'm sure she wished she had. At this point, Abigail had God. Like Joan, fear or no fear, she moved. Her insides may have been shaking, but her body was in motion.

And all the while, 1 Samuel 25:19 tells us, "But she did not tell her husband Nabal." Obviously, this detail is important for the Bible to mention it.

What do you think Abigail's reasoning is for not telling Nabal?

_____

_____

Maybe she was afraid Nabal would talk her out of it. Try to stop her. Make her feel foolish. She demonstrates that a confident woman doesn't have to blast her bravery to everyone. Abigail kept quiet and made her move.

Riding a donkey, she descended into a mountain ravine. That alone would be terrifying! She headed into her precarious situation out of desperation. She bringing her gifts. David bringing his swords. She is alone except for some servants, while he's followed by four hundred none-too-friendly men.

Coming around a bend, they meet. Abigail with her blessings, David with his "curse."

Based on 1 Samuel 25:21–22, in your own words record what David said to his men just prior to their departure.

_____

_____

Shaking on her donkey, as soon as Abigail saw David, she quickly got down and bowed low, her face to the ground.

What is the first trait Abigail displays to David?

_____

_____

True confidence is brave enough to be humble. Why would Abigail express such humility when she wasn't the one who messed up?

Though Abigail is bravely bold, she is not rude or in-your-face. In this ancient time, women's behavior was extremely limited, much like the women of Afghanistan during modern Taliban oppression. Physically, women were not allowed to leave the home of their husband without permission. They were normally restricted to roles of little or no authority. They were not allowed to talk to strangers.[35] Can you imagine what it would be like to not be allowed to even leave your home without consent?

Abigail asks David for permission to speak. She realizes David must listen to her if she is going to bring change. She would not have obtained his attention if she had not communicated in a respectful manner.

"Blame me; I didn't see your men come down! My husband is wicked; don't listen to him," Abigail implores.

Though our cultures are very different, what can you and I learn from the way Abigail handled this tension-filled situation?

_____

_____

_____

Abigail is smart. She tells David she knows God is with him. My paraphrase: "You are a good and wise man! Don't do this thing you're thinking about doing. You'll so regret it!"

David sees gentleness, goodness, faithfulness, and self-control in Abigail, and he responds respectfully (again, my words): "You're right! Thank you, Lord, for sending this woman to me!" After David accepts the gifts she has brought, Abigail heads home, having saved her entire household from death.

Abigail's wisdom doesn't stop at her dealings with just one man. After a long day saving her entire household, she enters her home to find her trouble-making spouse drunk as can be. But she holds her history-changing story for tomorrow.

She can wait. Confidence settles her and tells her that the right time will be the right time. Having been in communication with the Lord throughout this process, she could rest assured that the Lord would continue to show her His timing. There is no need to gush out her life-saving story, even if to relieve her own pent-up emotions.

When do you struggle to wait for the right time when it comes to speaking?

When Nabal is back in his sober mind, Abigail lets him in on the details. This woman to whom he possibly did not give the time of day had completely saved the day. Stunned at how his evil words almost destroyed their entire household, his terror turns into a heart attack. Ten days later, Nabal is dead. David, then, swooped up this woman of poise and made her his wife. Who ever said the Bible was boring?

Abigail lived out the truth of Proverbs 21:23: "Those who guard their mouths and their tongues keep themselves from calamity."

Yes, Abigail guarded her words, yet at the same time she was bold. She didn't let her status or her culture hold her back from making her move. She had something of value to give to David and she humbly offered it.

She had a word to deliver to Nabal and she waited for the perfect time to deliver it. Culture may look down on her for being a woman, but you would never know that by looking at Abigail. She didn't let her circumstances dictate her confidence.

Confidence isn't only for the powerful.

In fact, those who know they lack power need confidence all the more! God's confidence is for those of us unqualified to fix the mess we're in. (Whether our actions put us there or not!) Christ Confidence is extended to us when we have been pushed into a corner, afraid, yet having to find a way out of fear. Here, in this tight spot, our King comes for us, bringing His courage with Him. As this week's memory verse says, "God is within her, she will not fall; God will help her at break of day" (Psalm 46:5).

The sin of Nabal was pressing in on Abigail, bringing a judgment she did not deserve. She would pay for his sin if something did not change; if she did not receive grace from this one man, David.

And so it is with us. We, too, pay in this life if something doesn't change! Either as a result of our own sin or the sins of others, this place of desperation can all too easily push us to react to our trouble in a way we really don't want.

Romans 5:17 brings the hope we need: "For if, by the trespass of the one man, death reigned through that one man, how much more will those who receive God's abundant provision of grace and of the gift of righteousness reign in life through the one man, Jesus Christ!"

In Christ, we can reign. We can win! We do not have to give in to the pressure to react to pressure. We can have victory. In fact, we already have victory. *Reign* here in the Greek means "to reign as king, to become king."[36] If there is one thing that a king surely is it is confident. Why? He knows he has the power.

Whether we've been shoved into our situation because of the careless deeds of another (as Abigail was) or we're the ones who have pushed ourselves there by giving our emotions control (like Michal), God comes to our rescue the same! He comes, bringing His redemption as well as the wisdom and confidence we need to move forward.

Apply It

When we are faced with a serious situation, our first move needs to be to lean into God's Word to make us wise where we are simple. Psalm 19:7, 10 (ESV) says "The law of the Lord is perfect, reviving the soul; the testimony of the Lord is sure, making wise the simple . . . More to be desired are they than gold, even much fine gold; sweeter also than honey and drippings of the honeycomb."

All the gold in the world was not going to help Abigail buy her way out of this one. Yes, her gifts may have helped to soothe David's anger, but it wasn't her wealth that won him over. It was her confidence displayed on the foundation of wisdom.

In your life, do you need wisdom to know how and when to make your move? Take a moment to do a search, looking up phrases such as: What does the Bible have to say about raising children? What does the Bible have to say about my relationship with my husband? How can I handle my finances well, or what do I do with my anger? Choose a verse that pertains to your situation and begin to meditate on it so that it can soak into the deepest places of your heart.

★

The Signs Are All There

MEMORY VERSE: "God is within her, she will not fall; God will help her at break of day."—Psalm 46:5

AT THE END OF THE STORY of Abigail and David, 1 Samuel 25 says: "But Saul had given his daughter Michal, David's wife, to Paltiel son of Laish, who was from Gallim" (v. 44).

The story of Abigail ends with Michal, David's *other* wife.

Two princesses; two very different responses.

Both found themselves in situations that made them uncomfortable; more than uncomfortable. These situations embarrassed them and caused them fear.

Why did one woman draw David to herself while the other drove him away?

Luke 6:45 reveals the secret.

"A good person produces good things from the treasury of a good heart, and an evil person produces evil things from the treasury of an evil heart. *What you say flows from what is in your heart*" (Luke 6:45 NLT, emphasis mine).

The treasury of a good heart comes when we fill up our heart with the truth from God's Word, the truth of what He says about us. For instance:

"Let the king be enthralled by your beauty; honor him, for he is your lord" (Psalm 45:11).

"Open to me, my sister, my darling, my dove, my flawless one" (Song of Songs 5:2).

"The LORD *your God is with you, the Mighty Warrior who saves. He will take great delight in you; in his love he will no longer rebuke you, but will rejoice over you with singing"* (Zephaniah 3:17).

What caused the great contrast between Abigail and Michal when it came to the way they each responded to trouble? To embarrassment? To fear?

What was in their hearts.

Michal despised David *in her heart*. When it came time to speak to him, what came out was what was *in her heart*: animosity, hatred, agitation, hostility, hardness, and meanness. Based on her words, it would appear Michal allowed jealousy and fear of man to reside *in her heart*. Her thoughts about David determined the feelings she allowed to develop *in her heart*. Thoughts became feelings, which became actions. Her actions simply revealed her heart. She spoke out of her heart of insecurity, which drove others from her.

Our words are powerful. They have the ability to open doors for us or slam doors on us.

> ### Our words have the ability to open doors for us or slam doors on us.

But it's not just a matter of watching our words. Holding back our words is like holding back a flood with a sheet; insecurity and inferiority push us to relieve our pain.

No, it's not just a matter of watching our words. It's the matter of watching our heart.

Luke 6:45 reveals to us that words are really a heart issue, not a mouth issue. Why is that so?

_____

_____

Then there is the other princess. Based on what came out of Abigail's mouth, what can we discern was in her heart?

_____

_____

David was certainly drawn to Abigail, but it was not simply because she was beautiful. David said to Abigail, "Blessed be the LORD God of Israel, who sent you this day to meet me! Blessed be your discretion, and blessed be you, who have kept me this day from bloodguilt and from avenging myself with my own hand" (1 Samuel 25:32–33 ESV).

David calls out what he sees in Abigail: wisdom, strength, a strong self-esteem, confidence. David saw what was *in her heart*: the fruit of the Spirit, which is "love, joy, peace, forbearance, kindness, goodness, faithfulness, gentleness and self-control" (Galatians 5:22–23). Abigail didn't simply rise to the occasion that day. Her heart spilled out all that had been stored in it.

Could we look at Michal and Abigail and say they were each a product of their environment? Environment always plays a part in the people we might become. Michal and Abigail each had hardship. Michal grew up in a home with a jealous, revenge-filled father, who used her as a pawn. Abigail was married to a man who was "harsh and badly behaved" (1 Samuel 25:3 ESV). They would surely have both been the brunt of these men's ill-behavior.

What made the difference in how these women each responded when confronted with trouble in their homes?

We can go right back to Luke 6:45: "A good man brings good things out of the good *stored up* in his heart, and an evil man brings evil things out of the evil *stored up* in his heart. For the mouth speaks what the heart is full of" (emphasis mine). The difference was what each of these women had stored up in their heart.

To store up something requires intention.

The emergency announcement was all over the news: Due to the hurricane hitting the coast, our city could experience the aftermath. My job was to prepare: Store up water and food. In order to store it up, I had to intentionally get to the grocery store. Food and water were not going to just appear in our pantry. No matter how much I read about the storm online or watched the TV news tell of the warning, there was only one way I was going to store up for the storm: *I had to do something*.

If we desire to remain poised in even the worst of circumstances, we have to be intentional to store up the Word that will hold us in position and posture. We need to fill up our hearts with God's truth so that when temptations and trials hit like a tsunami, we're ready.

The storm of trouble hit both Abigail and Michal. What came out was what was stored up. For Abigail, what flowed was wisdom, confidence, humility, poise, bravery, and grace. For Michal, what gushed forth was foolishness, insecurity, pride, agitation, fear, and rudeness.

When we find our confidence in God and our hearts are *full* of trust, believing in the powers, trustworthiness, and reliability of our God, we can rest even in unrest. We don't have to manipulate or grasp at control in these times when fear and intimidation pound against us. We can choose, like Abigail, to lose no time in running to our God to bring up, not fear or terror, but what we have intentionally stored up *in our hearts*: confidence in our God.

We have to intentionally switch our attention from the everyday things consuming us, the thoughts pushing us toward negative, defeating feelings that come against our confidence in God. Those thoughts can come from so many places: insecurity in a relationship, fears for our future, and worries from our workplace. We need to seek the heart of Jesus to have a heart that trusts in Jesus.

> ## Seek the heart of Jesus to have a heart that trusts in Jesus.

Have you ever met a person who has a genuine love for other people? Instead of being focused on herself, she focuses on others, making those around her feel wanted, special, valued. This level of comfort with herself is something so beautiful!

Who comes to your mind when I say the word *confident*?

I immediately picture my friend Bonnie. When I first met her, she was so joyful, always looking on the bright side. I had never seen anything like it or anyone like her. I just knew it couldn't be real. No one could really be like that! But we've been friends now for more than fifteen years, and I have come to know that she is the real deal.

Tick. Tick. Tick. The waiting room clock drew my attention to the obvious: I wished we weren't there. Me in the silence and her surrounded by machines. Yesterday, laughing in the coffee shop had been a happier day for my friend and me. Now, I found myself anxiously waiting for her return with the nurse.

When I finally heard her voice coming down the hall, I was thrown off by her tone. What I heard was not that of a fearful woman facing the unknown. As she came into view, her expression was not that of a woman filled with uncertainty.

Her countenance radiated one thing: peaceful confidence. Complete and utter trust.

As I stood to offer my arm, hope spilled from her heart, "Before we go, please let me share with you the words Jesus has been whispering to me."

Taking a seat in that hospital lounge, my friend knew just where to go in God's Word at that moment. She had been intentionally filling her heart with the now familiar passage all week. Pouring her faith into me, it was all I could do to hold back the tears. *Wasn't I there to support her?* Yet, *her* words, filled with God's truth, were the life-giving ones that day.

Right before my very eyes, in the middle of the same hospital that had removed cancer just months before, my friend lived out Psalm 119:165: "Great peace have those who love your law, and nothing can make them stumble."

There is something otherworldly about being in the presence of one who has faced what we all may fear, who has touched God there and is no longer afraid of the pain this life might hold. I haven't experienced that level of fear before. I haven't paid the price to grasp the peace and poise Bonnie holds today. But I want it. I want the peace she has. I want my heart to be okay with anything that comes my way because my heart is peacefully resting in a God I know is good.

No matter what.

Jesus says He will give us a peace that surpasses all understanding (Philippians 4:7). I saw that peace. Literally saw it with my eyes in my gorgeous friend that morning. I witnessed the beauty that can only come when a woman is daily saturated in the Word of God. It's a beauty so gorgeous it's much more than what this world calls beautiful. It's confidence. It's certainty. It's what I want.

Most likely, I will not experience the exact pain Bonnie has been through. But I can still become valiant like my friend.

I know what to do to become like her.

I can become courageously confident by practicing life in God's presence daily, learning to love His law as the psalmist said.

Getting alone. Letting my heart go to that place, every day, where His Word soaks in because I let it. Setting aside all else, so His peace can seep into every inch of my heart. Allowing His peace to wedge out all fear. Building a foundation of faith that works fearlessness into me.

In spite of her pain, no, in the midst of her pain, my friend has exhibited a poise that can only be found in Jesus' peace.

Lord, make me like Bonnie. Make me like You.

Long before her diagnosis, Bonnie was preparing. She was pouring peace into her heart, so peace is what came out when she needed it most. She knew Jesus' promises: "I have told you these things, so that in me you may have peace. In this world you will have trouble. But take heart! I have overcome the world" (John 16:33).

Bonnie didn't know she would one day stare down a positive cancer test. Yet, as long as I have known her, every day she has soaked her heart in Jesus' promises that, in Him, we can overcome the world. She has filled her mind with this truth: "No, in all these things we are more than conquerors through Him who loved us" (Romans 8:37), and this one, too: "But thanks be to God, who in Christ always leads us in triumphal procession, and through us spreads the fragrance of the knowledge of him everywhere" (2 Corinthians 2:14 ESV).

So when she experienced trouble, the *fragrance of the knowledge of Him* spilled out of my beautiful friend. Not fear, bitterness, or self-pity. Was she perfect? No—our perfection, our full completion in Christ, is coming, but it is not yet here. "Not that I have already obtained this or am already perfect, but I press on to make it my own, because Christ Jesus has made me his own" (Philippians 3:12 ESV). Not perfect, but beautifully peaceful.

Michal and Abigail made clear the choice we have: Store up good and spill over good or allow meanness, bitterness, or insecurity to fill the space of our heart and spill the same. Let's choose to store up God's Word in our hearts, being intentional about what we allow in and what we allow to stay in our hearts.

Apply It

Are you intentionally filling your heart with "the fragrance of the knowledge of Jesus"? If so, how are you doing that?

_____

_____

_____

If you are not, here are a few ideas on how you can do this each day:

1. Read through the Bible in a year using a Bible reading plan.

2. Join a Bible study either at your church or online.

3. Set an alarm on your phone as a reminder to pray throughout the day.

4. Subscribe to a Bible app or devotional Bible study that you can read midday to refill your heart.

5. Ask a friend to become a prayer partner with you, touching base each day to pray for each other.

Visit www.Proverbs31.org for the tools for these steps plus many more!

★

Divine Difference

MEMORY VERSE: "God is within her, she will not fall; God will help her at break of day."—Psalm 46:5

MICHAL AND ABIGAIL. Two women, eventually married to the same man, but who couldn't have been more different.

Michal became bent out of shape when she thought her husband was making a fool of her. Abigail displayed fearlessness even while her husband *was* making a fool of her.

Paul reveals to us a key difference between these two women.

Digging Deeper

Let's dig into the third chapter of Paul's first letter to the Corinthians for some wisdom we can apply to ourselves and to understanding Michal and Abigail.

Read 1 Corinthians 3:1–3.

What does Paul say are signs of immaturity, and why?

_____

_____

_____

_____

Applying this Scripture to Michal, why do you think she lost it with her husband, David, in 2 Samuel 6:16?

_____

_____

Again, based on 1 Corinthians 3:1–3, why do you think Abigail didn't lose it with her husband, Nabal, in 1 Samuel 25?

_____

_____

Michal displayed both traits that Paul lists as signs of immaturity: quarreling and jealousy. She lacked maturity; she lacked wise confidence.

In 1 Corinthians 3:10–11 (ESV), Paul says we are to "each one take care how he builds . . . For no one can lay a foundation other than that which is laid, which is Jesus Christ."

What actions in Abigail reveal her foundation?

_____

_____

What actions in Michal reveal her foundation?

_____

_____

Abigail built her worth apart from her husband. Michal's actions display a woman whose worth was built on her husband and what others thought of him.

First Corinthians 3:13 goes on to say, "Their work will be shown for what it is, because the Day will bring it to light. It will be revealed with fire, and the fire will test the quality of each person's work."

Is there a time in your life when you have felt "under fire"? What was the result of this test?

_____

_____

Abigail and Michal experienced the "testing of the quality of their work." First Corinthians 3:14–15 reveals the consequences for the one who survives and the one who is "burned up". (Should you like to study further, you can read about the rest of Michal's life in 2 Samuel 6:21–23.)

As you look back, if the outcome of the test you experienced was one you would change if you could, in what way would you handle the test differently if you were to experience it again today?

_____

_____

_____

Several years ago, I had the honor of being asked to speak at a large women's ministry event. I couldn't believe it. I had "finally arrived." The fact that I even thought that reveals the biggest sin struggle in my life: pride. The event went well, and I felt certain it was an indication of what was to come. A few weeks afterward, I received a request to speak at a small gathering of moms for an entire weekend. The church anticipated approximately fifty women to attend. _Fifty? I've just spoken to over five hundred? A weekend is a big commitment for fifty people_, I thought. Wanting a second opinion to back up my belief, I asked my husband for his advice. I should have known God would use him to set me straight. In the kindest way, he confronted me: "Are you too big to speak to fifty, Lynn?" Of course, he was right, and I had fallen for pride once again.

Friends, I've been so prideful I've even been prideful enough to believe I'm no longer prideful! This sin trips me up again and again. The only way I am learning to build a confidence that doesn't cross over into pride or arrogance is to humble myself continually before God and other people. This means I practice James 5:16 often, confessing my sins to my spouse, my kids, my friends, and my Proverbs 31 teammates. I ask them to pray for me so that I change. Sharing my shortcomings with others humbles me and causes me to not have to keep up a façade of someone I am not.

And if I don't, well, God loves me enough to humble me!

When can pride mask itself as confidence or wisdom?

_____

_____

_____

The day I asked Greg for his input, he could have used 1 Corinthians 3:18–19 to give me the answer I needed: "Do not deceive yourselves. If any of you think you are wise by the standards of this age, you should become 'fools' so that you may become wise. For the wisdom of this world is foolishness in God's sight. As it is written: 'He catches the wise in their craftiness.'"

Why does God tell us we should become a fool?

_____

_____

_____

To some, Abigail may have looked like the fool, bowing with her face to the ground as she approached David. We know she was wise. She laid down her pride. She calmly headed to the source of her problem, all the while trusting God to contain the trouble ahead.

God's confidence isn't for the powerful.

In fact, those of us who know we lack power to change and to bring change need His confidence the most!

Now that we know the end of the story, we can look back and see what Abigail could not have seen, what she could not have known.

Even while she was living under the tyranny of Nabal, God was at work. He had a timetable. She may have felt day after day that she was suffering under the ugly leadership of one hard, harsh, difficult, stubborn, and stiff-necked man. *Didn't God see?* Her actions show she was a woman of knowledge, a woman to be respected. *Why did God allow her to be with this miserable man day after day after day?* She may have awoken each morning and felt as though life was continually the same; nothing was changing.

But change was coming. She just couldn't see it. She wouldn't have known that it would all change in a day.

While she was in pain, God was prompting. He was moving David into the desert. He was setting up the situation for His divine appointment. When Abigail went to meet David, she didn't arrive before David had left or after he had entered her estate. God had them meet in the ravine right on time.

While she was in pain, God was providing a plan for peace. He was setting into motion her eventual removal from her place of pain.

While she was in pain, God was preparing the penalty. Both David and Abigail could trust God to take care of Nabal. They didn't have to get involved, and thankfully they didn't! God is a God of justice. He would not allow Nabal to get away with the way he treated others. Proverbs 21:15 (ESV) says, "When justice is done, it is a joy to the righteous but terror to evildoers." I believe Abigail experienced joy, all right! "[David's] servants went to Carmel and said to Abigail, 'David has sent us to you to take you to become his wife'" (1 Samuel 25:40).

While she was in pain, God was positioning. He was positioning His protection. He was providing the right timing for Abigail and David's encounter so that David would not react in anger and possibly do something he would regret. David had shown restraint before (1 Samuel 24). God was positioning David to be protected for his own sake and for the protection of God's name in the community and country.

While Abigail was in pain, God was changing her position to change her perspective. Unlike the neighboring wives who might have known the intimate love of a husband, Abigail didn't know that kind of love. God was setting her up for something new.

God often needs to change our position so we can see things in a fresh way. Like David seeing this situation through Abigail's eyes.

Apply It

Might there be a situation in your life in which you are afraid you might look like the fool? That if you don't do something, it will all come crashing down and look like it was your fault?

We can clearly see from Michal and Abigail, there are two ways we can face this situation. Like Michal, we can attempt to take control. I don't know about you, but in my life, no good has ever come when I take the wheel. With the power of the Holy Spirit, we can listen for the wisdom He provides and move only as He gives us clarity.

God might not give you all the details so that you can see the end of your story, but He does want to give you confidence to be able to trust Him with it. Leaning into His wisdom and not our own can make the divine difference.

Write a prayer below, asking the Holy Spirit to give you the strength, power, and wisdom today to know His divine direction for your life.

Group Discussion Questions

Read this week's memory verse aloud as a group, or select an individual to do so: "God is within her, she will not fall; God will help her at break of day."—Psalm 46:5

1. Read 1 Samuel 18:7–8. Michal grew up witnessing her father lose his confidence due to his "questionable" relationship with David. How has your upbringing impacted how you handle relationships in question?

2. Based on this week's memory verse, how might Michal's actions have been different had she applied this truth when her confidence faltered as her relationship with David was in question?

3. When we fear people's approval over God's approval, we start looking to them to fill the insecurities and gaps in our hearts. And they just can't do it. God never created them to. Specifically, what are some of these insecurities and gaps in our lives we look to others to fill? How have you personally experienced this?

4. Refer back to 1 Samuel 25:4–42 and Abigail's example of fearless confidence and wisdom. What steps can you take on a daily basis to secure your confidence in Christ alone to make bold and wise moves?

5. As you wrap up your time together, share with each other who you feel most like today: Michal or Abigail. Pray over one another to let go of Michal responses and embrace Abigail-type confidence in the Lord.

If you took the step to begin a new life with Jesus today, please be sure to share this wonderful news with your small group leader so she can celebrate with you!

WEEK SIX

Martha & Mary

WHEN CONFIDENCE IS IN DOUBT

★

PRAYER: *Jesus, life rarely goes as planned. Teach me during this last week that when I experience the troubles You said would come my way, I do not have to abandon the confidence I have gained in You. Instead, help me to remember who You have proven Yourself to be to me and who You are in me. You are my confidence. In Jesus' name, Amen.*

MEMORY VERSE: "Now, little children, abide in him, so that when he appears we may have confidence and not shrink from him in shame at his coming."—1 John 2:28 (ESV)

★

Meet Martha

AS A YOUNG MOTHER AT TWENTY-SEVEN, I began watching the ugly thing called cancer come at my father again and again. I wondered at his strength during those trips to chemotherapy. A gentle smile would come across the face of few words but one that had just discovered the power of saying, "I love you, too." Sickness has a way of drawing out the deepest within us, and my father was no exception. He continued to love us the way he always had, preparing for our needs right up to the end. Planning his funeral, picking out his plot; he did what he had always done, take care of us.

As my father started losing his battle for life just days before my thirty-second birthday, I experienced my own *if you had been here, Jesus.* Sometimes, when the life in jeopardy is so very close to our own, our humanness cannot process why God would allow that life to be cut short. *Why would You allow us to be without him? My kids will never get to know their grandpa. Who will stand by my mom as she grows older?* "I don't understand" thoughts would onslaught me with no warning. I spent the night of my birthday next to his hospital bed wondering at the turn my life was taking as I cared for the one who had spent his life taking care of me.

Not having close friends who had lost a parent or understood my approaching loss, I didn't know where to turn for comfort. I tried to fathom life without my strong and stable father. Though a quiet man, he had been a rock for us all.

I imagine these were some of the pains that the sisters of Bethany experienced as their only brother's body lay in the tomb. The Bible doesn't mention any males in their family other than their brother, Lazarus—no dad, no other brothers, no husbands, or sons.

Now, it's just the two of them. It's no wonder Martha greeted Jesus with her criticism, "Lord, if you had been here . . ."

Loving Jesus doesn't mean we get to skip hard things in life. It just takes a day in a life to find this is true. Disappointments sometimes replace dreams. Unrealistic expectations of ourselves and others crowd out the happiness we hoped to experience.

It was no different for the sisters of Bethany. In the middle of learning who Jesus really is, life crashed against their blossoming faith.

Some of you may have already met the sister duo of Mary and Martha of Bethany. Most teachings on these two don't shine light all that favorably on Martha. Typecast as the "doer," all too often Martha's personal faith and love for Jesus fall under the shadow of her sister Mary. Might we be missing something about the other sister?

Both Mary *and* Martha loved Jesus. Let's look for Martha's love and faith to shine in today's study.

The passage we're about to read is not the first time the family of Bethany is mentioned in the Bible. Luke 10:38–42 tells the most familiar story of Jesus and His disciples being invited into Martha's home for the first time. (If you haven't read about this encounter before, you might choose to begin your study today there, where the sisters' relationship with Jesus begins.)

Digging Deeper

Let's read the second recorded encounter Martha has with Jesus in John 11:1–27. Note below anything that stands out or seems abnormal to you in this account.

_____

_____

_____

My heart goes out to Martha. I understand her broken heart.

Maybe Martha wondered as she looked at Lazarus's lifeless body, "If Jesus loved us, why would He have allowed *this*? He knows we need our brother." This tragedy could have easily been prevented if Jesus would have simply come when the sisters called for Him.

Jesus hadn't followed their plan or met their expectations whatsoever.

Jesus had His reasons for stalling. He clearly explains in verse 4, "It is for God's glory so that God's Son may be glorified through it."

Who were the first persons that Jesus mentions as needing to see this upcoming miracle (v. 15)?

_____

_____

Who was *not* in Jesus' presence when He gave this explanation?

_____

_____

Jesus gave His purpose for Lazarus's illness and subsequent death, but Mary and Martha were not there to hear His answer. Sometimes, even if we do hear His words, they are not the ones we *want* to hear.

We just want our pain fixed.

223

Verses 5–6 (ESV) go on to say, "Now Jesus loved Martha and her sister and Lazarus. So, when he heard that Lazarus was ill, he stayed two days longer in the place where he was."

What are your thoughts on what appears to be a contradiction: Jesus loved this family, yet when He heard Lazarus was sick, He stayed where He was for two more days?

_____

_____

_____

Jesus "wanted them to learn that His delays are not denials; that He knows the exact moment to display His power."[37] Remember during Week 4 when I said confidence is often built in uncomfortable environments? If Jesus had come to this family's immediate rescue, there would have been no reason for the sisters to develop and exercise confidence.

The sisters had sent for Jesus and had offered a prayer of sorts. "Lord, he whom you love is ill" (v. 3 ESV). They had confidence that He would hear them. They were right; He did.

What does 1 John 5:14–15 reassure us concerning our prayers?

_____

_____

My heart needs this hope and comfort today—this faith booster. Confidence that we can ask anything according to His will and He hears us, powers our prayers.

Look up Matthew 7:7–8 and fill in the blanks below:

Ask, and _____.

Seek, and _____.

Knock, and _____.

Who does Matthew 7:7–8 say is excluded from receiving this promise?

Jesus leaves no room for doubt. The answer to our prayer . . . will happen. Period.

Ask . . . and it will.

Seek . . . and it will.

Knock . . . and it will.

This is the faith-push that empowers us. When disappointment and discouragement deplete me, God's directives restore me.

> *When disappointment and discouragement deplete me, God's directives restore me.*

When Martha heard that Jesus was coming, she went out to meet Him. She may not have understood what took Him so long, but even in her lack of understanding and her disappointment and discouragement, Martha drew close to Jesus. Her faith caused her to go out and meet Him. Just as our memory verse this week, 1 John 2:28, says, when He appeared, Martha had confidence and did not shrink away from Him in shame at His coming.

What does James 4:8 tell us will happen when we choose to draw near to Jesus?

How does this encourage you?

_____

_____

As Martha converses with Jesus, she isn't in denial about what has happened or how she feels. In fact, her beginning statement reveals sadness, disappointment, even frustration. "If you had been here, my brother would not have died." Yet from this place of not fully understanding, she begins her next faith-filled statement with the powerful conjunction: *but*. "But I *know* that even now God will give you whatever you ask" (John 11:22, emphasis mine).

I know.

There is Martha's confidence. You can see her fully trusting. You can hear her belief in His power. She knows she can rely on Him. Even if she doesn't understand, faith and trust have caused her to draw toward Jesus, not pull away from Him. Confidence draws us closer to Jesus; insecurity drives us away.

> ### *Confidence draws us closer to Jesus; insecurity drives us away.*

When our mind tells us, *Jesus has disappointed me, let me down, or not come through*, our lack of self not rooted in Christ tells us to run from Him. As. Fast. As. We. Can. We've heard the story again and again; maybe it's our own. *I trusted God, and when He didn't come through, I walked away.*

Insecurity could have told Martha: *Jesus doesn't truly love you. If He did, He would have come.* Insecurity leans into doubt, telling us our fears are validated and true.

Instead, Martha voices her faith: "But even now I know that whatever you ask from God, God will give you" (John 11:22 ESV), and the bedrock of her confidence is exposed. She has already fixed in her mind the truth of who Jesus is, and that truth is what she stands on in the middle of her sorrow. Her circumstances are not dictating what she thinks or what she knows. She knows Jesus is God's Son and that God will give His son whatever He asks. She didn't grasp why He didn't come before Lazarus died. Her lack of understanding, though, doesn't change the fact that she knows who Christ is.

Did she get what she wanted? No.

Was she happy about it? Absolutely not.

"But *even now* I know . . ." (ESV)

Even now. Even now that my loved one has died.

The Lord can empower *us* to also say: even now.

➤ Even now that I am unemployed and broke.

➤ Even now that my marriage has failed.

➤ Even now that my future looks bleak.

➤ Even now that my child is running from You.

➤ Even now when I am depressed and my mind is confused.

➤ Even now that _____. (You fill in the blank.)

You and I, like Martha, can say, "I know even now. I perceive as truth and fix in my mind that You are who You say You are. From my past experiences with Your faithfulness, I know that this present situation does not change one thing about You."

We can *choose* to believe Ephesians 3:20–21 (ESV): "Now to him who is able to do far more abundantly beyond all that we ask or think, according to the power at work within us, to him be glory in the church and in Christ Jesus throughout all generations, forever and ever. Amen." Is this an easy choice? For sure, it is not. It is the decision, though, that will lead us to hope, a hope that will not disappoint.

Jesus, I know You are able. Say that out loud. *Jesus, I know You are able.* Continue to read these statements aloud: *You are with me. You will never forsake me. Nothing changes because You didn't come when I wanted You to come. I can put my trust in You who are able* before *You have done it.*

Continually thanking Him for all He has done, before He has done it, fuels my faith to keep believing.

> ## Continually thanking Him for all He has done, before He has done it, fuels my faith to keep believing.

I have in my office a print given to me by my friend, Stacey, with the words: EVEN IF . . . I STILL WILL. It is taken from Habakkuk 3:17–19:

> *"Though the fig tree should not blossom,*
> *nor fruit be on the vines,*
> *the produce of the olive fail*
> *and the fields yield no food,*
> *the flock be cut off from the fold*
> *and there be no herd in the stalls,*
> *yet I will rejoice in the* Lord;
> *I will take joy in the God of my salvation.*
> God, *the Lord, is my strength;*
> *he makes my feet like the deer's,*
> *he makes me tread on my high places."* (ESV)

Such a powerful statement of faith! Even if . . . I still will.

Sorrow from a variety of sources can push on our soul, squeezing out what is inside—confidence or insecurity. Standing on the confidence we find in Christ, we, too, can say, "Even if . . . I still will."

Martha may have been grappling with a cacophony of negative emotions in her heart and mind, but she still chose to draw near to Jesus. Her Christ Confidence held her up.

Apply It

Take a moment to write below Habakkuk 3:17–19, adapting it to your own "though it" phrases. I'll share my first line with you for an example: "Though the healing should not come . . ."

_____

_____

_____

_____

_____

_____

End with reading aloud to the Lord what you have written, making it a declaration of your own, "I still will."

★

The Power of Words

MEMORY VERSE: "Now, little children, abide in him, so that when he appears we may have confidence and not shrink from him in shame at his coming."—1 John 2:28 (ESV)

I WASN'T SURE WHY, but I just knew the texts I was receiving were not for me. Suddenly I received a call from my daughter: "Mom, are you getting my texts?" she asked.

I sure was. Madi's phone was receiving my texts, while mine received hers. Somehow the cell service we share had crossed our phone numbers. Though neither of us had said anything embarrassing, we both had the same reaction: *What if . . .?*

Until they could figure out what was going wrong, we were both going to be paying close attention to our words.

Digging Deeper

When we left Jesus and Martha, the two of them were having a powerful conversation in John 11. Martha had just told Jesus, "But I know that even now God will give you whatever you ask" (v. 22). Jesus goes on to give Martha the Truth on which she can fix her faith.

Write out John 11:25–26 below. With what question does Jesus end His declaration?

_____

_____

How does Martha's response solidify Jesus' statement in her own life?

_____

_____

Martha voiced her faith, "I believe." So much is packed into those two words. It's Martha's own "even if . . . I will still."

The words we say contain much more power than we realize. Martha's own "I believe" stabilized her faith in this shaky hour. Maybe Martha had learned the potential of words from passages in Proverbs she had learned as a child.

Proverbs 4:23 challenges us to keep our heart with all vigilance, for from it flows the springs of life. Then in Luke 6:45, Jesus uses similar language concerning our heart and words.

Look up Luke 6:45. What correlation does Jesus make between our heart and our words?

_____

_____

Our words reveal so much: Is our heart filled with faith and confidence or doubt and insecurity?

What does Proverbs 12:13 say happens when the righteous use their words wisely?

_____

_____

The words I say have the power to reinforce my Christ Confidence as well as tear it down. I need to run the words of my mouth past His word in my heart before I speak!

> *I need to run the words of my mouth past His word in my heart before I speak.*

Knowing just how powerful my words can be, I want to use them to bring good—into my life and into the life of others. God's Word spells out how we can do just that:

1. Bring Life.

Proverbs 18:21 tells us. "The tongue has the power of life and death, and those who love it will eat its fruit."

I remind myself continually that my words have the ability to breathe new life into my heart *and* into the hearts of others. At the same time, my words have the power to bring a death blow.

Lord, help me to bring life with my words today.

2. Bring encouragement.

Paul encourages us in Ephesians 4:29: "Let no corrupting talk come out of your mouths, but only such as is good for building up, as fits the occasion, that it may give grace to those who hear" (ESV).

Corrupting means "bad, rotten, decayed; unwholesome."[38] If what I am about to say spoils or taints my heart and mind or those of someone listening, it's a no-go.

Lord, empower me to bring encouragement and build another person up today.

3. Bring healing.

Every day brings with it plenty of opportunities for hardships and hurt. When first we run our words by the wisdom of God, we can be a person who brings healing to our own heart as well as to others, rather than wounding. "There is one whose rash words are like sword thrusts, but the tongue of the wise brings healing" (Proverbs 12:18 ESV).

Lord, use me and my words to deliver healing to a hurting heart today, even when that heart is my own.

4. Bring health.

Is there someone I can bring a smile to, add a bit of sweetness to their day? If you have a good thought come to mind, say it! It is so easy to say, "What a great outfit!" or "You have a beautiful smile." Sharing some sweetness with another can give their confidence a boost and make us feel good as well!

"Gracious words are like a honeycomb, sweetness to the soul and health to the body" (Proverbs 16:24 ESV).

Lord, open my eyes to the one to whom I can speak sweetness today!

5. Bring a soft answer.

Not every conversation we have can be wrapped up in a pink bow. Just look at these serious conversations between Jesus and the sisters. If our conversations are always on the surface, positive and never hard, it means we aren't being honest, we're doing some stuffing, or both! (Not that I've ever done that!)

Mary and Martha were honest with Jesus with their thoughts and feelings. Love made Him a safe place to be real. We, too, can be raw, real, and vulnerable with those who are safe. We can do so in a way that is kind, gracious, and gentle. Mary and Martha didn't use sarcasm or shouting to get their point across to their Savior. A respectful delivery of an honest word can help us to be heard.

> *A respectful delivery of an honest word can help us to be heard.*

"A soft answer turns away wrath, but a harsh word stirs up anger" (Proverbs 15:1 ESV).

Lord, when I want to raise my voice and feel heard, remind me to speak confidently, yet respectfully today.

Martha may have been struggling on this sorrow-filled day with not understanding Jesus' choices or His ways, but she harnessed those emotions and did not allow them to control her. Truth triumphed over her tongue. Her confidence in Christ held her up as she and Jesus went to her sister, Mary.

Mary had chosen to stay at home in her sorrow, not coming with her sister to greet Jesus.

Mary, I get you. Waiting to see if Jesus would come. Waiting to see if He would want you. And when your sister comes to you in private saying, "The Teacher is here and is calling for you" (John 11:28 ESV), you go running.

Me, too. Me, too.

Read John 11:28–37 for Mary's part in Lazarus' testimony.

Just as we have been quick to judge Martha's get-it-done personality, it would be so easy for us to do the same toward Mary. Why did she wait? Was she pouting or privately grieving?

Waiting for Jesus to come doesn't make Mary bad. When she was called, she didn't refuse to be consoled. She went, taking her grief to her Savior. Though she came broken, she *still came.* She brought her rawness. She brought her disillusionment. She brought all of her and fell at the feet of Jesus.

Like Martha, Mary begins her conversation with Jesus the same way, "Lord, if you had been here, my brother would not have died" (v. 32). I'm guessing the sisters had been asking each other for days: *Where is He?*

How did Jesus respond to Mary's rebuke?

_____

_____

I so want to learn to be compassionate like Jesus. He was moved by her pain. My own get-it-done personality is all too often the opposite of compassionate. Fear of losing control and falling in a pit of complaining, my mind commands me to just keep going. *Don't let your feelings get out of control! Don't feel too deeply, you might not get out!* My personality tells me to buck up and expect others to do the same. All too often, I know I've come across as unfeeling, when what others need from me most is to simply validate the way they feel. I don't have to be fearful that seeking to understand how someone feels means I am going to slip into the sin of grumbling. Like Jesus, I can listen and bring my love and comfort to their pain and hurt.

Take a moment to really look at Jesus. Let's slow down and sense the tension He feels with the sisters and the sorrow He carries in His own heart. "Deeply moved in his spirit and greatly troubled" (John 11:33 ESV), He does not struggle to show His compassionate love. Jesus has no fear of His emotions. The shortest verse in the Bible may very well be one of the most powerful: "Jesus wept" (v. 35 ESV).

Being confident doesn't mean being emotionless. Being confident doesn't mean I stand back so I don't fall apart. Confidence doesn't require me to always have everything together.

Jesus is overcome with emotion as He makes His way to the tomb of His beloved friend. And there, "groaning deeply again" (v. 38 ISV), He voices a command: "Take away the stone" (v. 39). Practical Martha steps up, reminding Jesus: Lazarus' body has been in the tomb for four days. He is going to stink!

Isn't that usually the way it is with miracles? The situation becomes beyond stinky before our Savior steps in? Jesus knows that if our circumstances are anything short of severe, we'd explain away His miracle!

Jesus reminds Martha of His promise, "Did I not tell you that if you believe, you will see the glory of God?" (v. 40)

In what direction did Jesus set His eyes before the miracle took place (vv. 41–42)?

Jesus didn't look toward the tomb where Lazarus' body was. He looked *up*, setting His eyes not on the problem but on the Answer. He was confident about where His power, and His answer, came from. Let's look again at Jesus' prayer.

Write below the first sentence of Jesus' prayer in John 11:41. In what tense is this sentence written: past, present, or future?

What can you deduce about Jesus and His Father based on these words?

Jesus said, "Thank you that you have already heard me," yet this is the first time He is praying in this passage. His words reveal that He and His Father had been talking all along. Jesus and His Father were in continual communion. On the journey to Bethany, they were talking. From the meeting with the sisters to the tomb, they were conversing. When Jesus commanded the stone to be removed, He knew His Father had already heard Him because they had already been communing with each other. As His daughters, we also have this open door of communion available to us. No matter where we are, how we feel, or what we are facing, He is with us and just waiting for dialogue to begin.

Did you catch that word of confidence again: *knew*? Jesus knew His father heard Him. "I knew that you always hear me, but I said this on account of the people standing around, that they may believe that you sent me" (11:42 ESV). Jesus spoke this prayer not to build His own faith but for the benefit of others—the power of the spoken word.

Martha knew Jesus *could.* Jesus knew God *would.*

And He did. "The dead man came out, his hands and feet wrapped with strips of linen, and a cloth around his face. Jesus said to them, 'Take off the grave clothes and let him go'" (v. 44).

Finally, at chapter's end, the reason for all this physical and emotional pain was revealed: "Therefore many of the Jews who had come to visit Mary, and had seen what Jesus did, believed in him" (v. 45). God had chosen to use the trial of the Bethany family as an opportunity to introduce many to Himself. While some believed for the first time, the faith of Lazarus, Mary, and Martha grew deeper roots than ever before. So did that of the disciples.

Through the conversations between Jesus and the sisters, we can see the power of our words. They reveal so much about what is in our hearts—our faith and confidence as well as our doubt and insecurity. We can use the power of words in our own lives to solidify our confidence and to encourage others to look for miracles as well.

Apply It

Look back at the five ways we can use the power of our words for good (pages 233–234). Thinking of your own current struggles, choose one of the five ways and below write how you can use your words today to bring good into your life and the life of another.

_____

_____

Lord, I see how the words I say not only reveal my confidence or lack of it but also impact my confidence as well. Please empower me today, Holy Spirit, to run the words of my mouth past Your Word in my heart before I speak. In Jesus' name, Amen.

★

Back for a Visit

MEMORY VERSE: "Now, little children, abide in him, so that when he appears we may have confidence and not shrink from him in shame at his coming."—1 John 2:28 (ESV)

FOLLOWING LAZARUS'S RESURRECTION, the narrative continues in John 11 as the chief priests and Pharisees plot to kill Jesus. As John 12 opens, Jesus' death draws closer, with Passover just six days away. During this time, Jesus leans into the company of His familiar friends—Lazarus, Martha, and Mary.

The three host a dinner in Jesus' honor. Martha again uses her gifts and talents, giving hospitality to their guests, while Lazarus relaxes at the table.

Digging Deeper

Read John 12:3–8.

Many pieces of this story can be hard for us to relate to because of the ancient time in which it took place. Re-create the story for our modern day by thinking of something expensive and

extravagant you might give as a gift. What would be an unusual and uncomfortable setting for this gift to be given?

Too often I skim over story details because they seem inapplicable to my life, and in the process I miss so much meaning found in those details. Modernizing the story takes it from AD 30–33 to today.

Through the death and resurrection of Lazarus, Mary had again seen the very thing that drew her to Jesus: His great love. She watched Him weep. She received His compassion. She witnessed His devotion to her family.

Now, Mary could contain herself no longer. She couldn't just be a recipient of love. She had to be a giver. She needed to show her gratitude and appreciation for the miracle He had just performed for her family.

No ordinary gift would do. It must be the very best, *her* very best.

While anointing the head with oil was a mark of respect sometimes paid by a host to his guests, including the feet absolutely would not be.[39] It was a humble, if not humiliating, act. Yet Mary's "dirty work" filled the home with the fragrance of her sacrifice.

Mary knew her culture's rules, just as you and I know ours. She was very aware that her place was not at the feet of Jesus; women were not "allowed" to learn directly from a teacher. She knew it was inappropriate to use expensive perfume in such an extravagant way let alone use her hair of all things to wipe His feet. It didn't matter what others thought. Mary loved Jesus. A peace had settled in her soul as she decided what she would do to honor her Love.

Mary may have felt scared of the crowd surrounding Jesus as she approached Him, but she didn't hold back. Confidence in the love of Jesus compelled her. As she walked out in obedience to what her spirit was compelling her to do, her confidence increased. Obedience is a confidence builder.

Obedience is a confidence builder.

As Mary lovingly demonstrated her unguarded and vulnerable love for the Son of God, she found herself under attack. Where God moves, the enemy moves.

Where God moves, the enemy moves.

My favorite way to spend time with the Lord is first thing in the morning. When all is quiet, I fill my heart with His Word. In the middle of one of these moments, a memory popped in my mind. Painful and hurt-filled, this memory from years ago, involved me unknowingly letting someone down. She felt I had failed her. She said my failure was an indication that I was unqualified, and she let others know what she thought as well. Why did this memory come back now after so many years? I thought I was well past that blow.

As I reflected for a few moments, the Holy Spirit helped me understand. I had recently made a new move with the Lord, saying yes to an assignment that appeared beyond my qualification. Once I saw my returned memory in that light, it made sense. The enemy would remind me what he had tried to drill into me years before: *You don't have what it takes.*

With God's help, I had finally put that failure behind me. I had found a new level of confidence by becoming more dependent on Jesus and therefore was stronger than ever before. I had found freedom in who God says I am, not another person's report.

Discovering confidence in our God is not a once-and-done process. In fact, it will be ongoing until the day we see Him face-to-face. As long as we are on this earth and "the devil prowls around like a roaring lion looking for someone to devour" (1 Peter 5:8), there will be opportunities for our confidence to be attacked and for us to turn to our God for His help.

Second Corinthians 3:16–18 tells us why the enemy keeps coming after us. Read this passage and then hone in on the last verse, looking for the reason he keeps up his attacks. Share this below.

_____

_____

_____

The enemy hates God's glory, this radiance, this confidence, which is the Holy Spirit Himself in us. This is why the enemy tries to crush our glory, and one of his main tactics is diversion—getting our eyes off of Jesus.

This day, as Mary anointed Jesus with oil, where was all of the attention going (John 12:4–6)?

_____

Mary's heart and eyes were on one person: Jesus. As her perfume drifted through the air, others turned to Jesus, from whom this lovely fragrance emanated. Satan couldn't stand it. Through Judas, he tried to push Mary and all who were witnessing her love to look anywhere but on the King of Glory. Push her to become self-conscious and look to herself.

Push Mary to draw attention to herself through her reaction. Push others to doubt Mary's sincerity and look to judge her. Push the entire room to validate Judas and look to exalt her accuser. Anywhere but looking upon Jesus.

The day my failure came to mind, the enemy might have thought he was being oh-so-sneaky. He knows we reflect the beauty, goodness, and love of *his* enemy, Jesus. He will do all he can to push down this glory, and he will use any tactic, including our past failures and fears.

Have you experienced an accusing action or past memory come over you right when you were in the middle of pointing others to Jesus? Were you able to recognize the source of this doubt as it came against your confidence?

_____

_____

_____

When the enemy presses in on us, pushing us to abandon God's gift of confidence to us, we must remind him of God's Word.

Look up 2 Corinthians 4:6–7. In verse 6, what has God caused to happen?

_____

_____

I just want to jump up and down and shout *Yes! Yes! Yes!* Yes, we don't deserve to shine His light. Yes, we are not worthy. That is the whole plan—to put His glory in us so that what is seen is not us. It's Jesus.

Continue reading in 2 Corinthians 4:8–15.

Paul lists many terrible things that try to wipe out our confidence. But he also tells us exactly why we can continue to hold on to our confidence in Christ and never lose it, no matter what! All we have is built on the life of Jesus in us.

What does Paul say is an indicator of our belief?

_____

_____

There it is again, the power of words.

What clear instruction does Paul give in 2 Corinthians 4:16–18 to take this passage to a level of practical, day-in-day-out application?

_____

_____

Mary was certainly hard pressed, crushed, perplexed, persecuted, and struck down by the blow the enemy delivered via Judas.

Judas in this story represents those who care how they look in the eyes of others, how every situation impacts them. They never see what is truly valuable, *who* is truly valuable. Judas didn't see in Mary's actions the value of love, honor, and respect for the One who deserved every drop of her perfume. Judas became a pawn in the hand of the enemy.

Mary made her move toward Jesus and the enemy made his.

Just because you make your move, in no way does that mean the enemy intends to stop making his. Even while you are in the very act of advancing, the enemy will try to stop you.

Mary drew close to honor Jesus, *no matter what it cost her.* The enemy hates when God is glorified. He hates when Jesus receives what the enemy himself craves: glory and honor that does not belong to him. He attempts to use people to divert glory being given to Jesus. He speaks through Jesus' own disciple to distract, detract, and destroy the deity of Christ. He will stop at nothing to defame Jesus.

The last thing Satan wants is for you to receive what you need: healing. The last thing he wants is for you to receive what you want: abundant life. The last thing he wants is for you to experience what God has for you: your potential and His glory.

How did Mary respond to this attack? Look again at John 12.

_____

_____

She doesn't, does she? So fixated on Christ, nothing—not even the evil words of Judas—can cause her to look away. Instead of defending herself, Mary lets her Defender defend her.

And He does. "Leave her alone" is His command (v. 7).

Maybe as you read those words, like me you thought, _I wish someone had said that for me._ Jesus' words of protection stirred up an old childhood remembrance, caused by a neighbor boy. Painful and shameful at one time, I wish someone had known and come to my defense.

This wounding, which has a statistic that is staggering for those of us who are female, is sorrowfully common. Abuse, in its many forms, impacts our identity and the way that we see ourselves no matter when the pain was inflicted.

Maybe you would be willing to join me in an exercise I did when I read Jesus' defense of Mary. I shut my eyes and pictured Jesus doing the same thing for me that He did for Mary. Coming to my rescue, He commanded, "Leave her alone." I've never done that before, but after I did, I had a very real sense: I don't have to go back to that place in my past again.

Painful encounters, whether they come from strangers, friends, or family, damage our confidence. Jesus wants to restore our ability to trust and believe in His protection.

Mary knew Jesus loved her. "Having loved his own who were in the world, he loved them to the end" (John 13:1). Yes, Mary knew that it was true. She heard it in His words; saw love in His acts. Her heart was convinced and when a heart is fully convinced that it is loved, confidence floods in. She didn't care what others thought or what others said; her only desire was for her Jesus to know she loved Him.

When a heart is fully convinced that it is loved, confidence floods in.

Apply It

Take a moment to reflect on a time when the enemy attempted to steal God's glory in you. Maybe, like me, that time involved an abusive situation. Maybe he tried to steal from you with a return of a memory. It may have occurred, when like Mary, you were pointing others to your Jesus.

The enemy does not have the right or the power to steal from us what Jesus has already died to give us: freedom and healing. Take this time to once again thank Jesus that He is the King of Glory and deserves all our worship. Sing a song that speaks of His greatness. Praise Him for His goodness. In whatever way your heart desires, express your thankfulness for all He has done and for all He is to you. You'll be reminding the enemy: You have no place here.

As our memory verse says, "Now, little children, abide in him, so that when he appears we may have confidence and not shrink from him in shame at His coming" (1 John 2:28 ESV).

DAY FOUR

★

Love Continues

MEMORY VERSE: "Now, little children, abide in him, so that when he appears we may have confidence and not shrink from him in shame at his coming."—1 John 2:28 (ESV)

MARY DEMONSTRATED TO JESUS in a tangible way how she loved Him. In John 13, He would do the same for His disciples.

As their Passover dinner wrapped up, Jesus prepared. Laying aside His outer garment, He was doing more than putting down a piece of clothing. He exposed His humble heart. As He wrapped a towel around His waist and poured water into a basin, He put on vulnerability as well. The washing of His disciples' naked feet and the teaching He shared with His humble actions revealed the innermost part of who He was. Unafraid, He performed this service confidently because He knew who He was: God's own Son.

Digging Deeper

Read John 13:1–17. As you read this passage, think about how Jesus serves His disciples. Write character traits you see in Him that you want to see in yourself.

_____

_____

Verse 3 reveals a word we have been seeing over and over in this chapter: *knew*. "Jesus knew that the Father had put all things under his power, and that he had come from God and was returning to God; so he got up from the meal, took off his outer clothing, and wrapped a towel around his waist" (vv. 3–4).

Jesus *knew*. He knew He was God's Son and that He was returning to His Father. He knew this was His last night of life as it had been, the last night before His death. He was confident His Father would carry out His plan in His way. There was no need for Jesus to force anything. When you know who has the power and all your trust is in that power, you don't have to grasp for control.

In the NIV translation, at the beginning of verse 4, there is the conjunction *so*. I think of this word as a gate of sorts. The action in verse 4 hinged on, or was opened, by the statement in verse 3.

Explain why verse 3 was important with regard to Jesus' actions in verse 4.

_____

_____

In Jesus, we see that humility and confidence are never at odds with each other.

> *Humility and confidence are never at odds with each other.*

Not so with humility and pride. Superiority and self-importance can often be mistaken for confidence. This type of warped confidence has its full trust and belief in the powers or reliability of ourselves, creating an elevated and unhealthy sense of self-worth. When our foundation is constructed on our own gifts and talents, Christlike humility cannot be created in us. That instability is not the place for one of God's children, for as Proverbs 16:18 states, "Pride goes before destruction, a haughty spirit before a fall." I could write another book about the times I have lived that verse out!

Jesus knew His own worth as God's Son. This was the basis from which He lived and the place from which we can live. Our foundation as His children won't crumble.

Read Philippians 2:1–11.

The first part of verse 3 gives the basis for how the Son of God could wash feet. What motivated Jesus as He served?

_____

_____

How does Paul say we should emulate Christ (v. 5)?

_____

_____

How does Paul say Jesus demonstrated His humility (vv. 7–8)?

_____

_____

Back to the Upper Room, Peter, the doer, struggled with Jesus' service. He didn't want to be washed by Jesus; he wanted to do the washing. Yet Jesus tells him no; this is the time for you to rest; the time to move will come.

Reread John 13:12–17 (ESV) below. Circle Jesus' instructions to us, a command that will require the deepest level of confidence.

> "When he had washed their feet and put on his outer garments and resumed his place, he said to them, 'Do you understand what I have done to you? You call

me Teacher and Lord, and you are right, for so I am. If I then, your Lord and Teacher, have washed your feet, you also ought to wash one another's feet. For I have given you an example, that you also should do just as I have done to you. Truly, truly, I say to you, a servant is not greater than his master, nor is a messenger greater than the one who sent him. If you know these things, blessed are you if you do them.'"

Is there a part of you that feels like you didn't see this coming? The biggest reason I am developing confidence in my life is to . . . wash feet?

Jesus' words are so convicting. He fills me with Himself, with Christ Confidence, so I can wash feet. So I can serve others. He fills me with confidence so that I can do what no one else would want to do because there is no applause attached. I can feed the hungry—the hungry at my dinner table at 6:00 p.m. and the hungry of the homeless in my city. I can help the helpless—my aging parents with their housework and those in India who have no hope for upward mobility. I can wake before dawn to put in a load of laundry or turn a high school into a sanctuary.

I've read this passage so many times, yet I am struck anew. Jesus, the Son of God. Jesus, the name above all names and the One before whom every knee will bow and every tongue confess —this Jesus . . . washed His servants' feet. The One who should have been served, who had every right to be served, served instead.

I am challenged to ask myself: *Is this my motivation for becoming more confident . . . so I can serve others?*

Does this revelation feel anticlimactic? Does it seem that here, at the end of our study, as Jesus is preparing to die, we should reach some pinnacle requiring great boldness?

Such is God's ways and His kingdom, upside down and always challenging our way of thinking. Constantly rubbing up against my pride and my self-serving heart, He lovingly shines the light on my motives.

We shouldn't be surprised. It's not the first time He has alluded to this hard message.

Read the mother of Zebedee's sons request in Matthew 20:20–28. What does Jesus say is the key to being great in His kingdom?

_____

_____

"Not so with you. Instead, whoever wants to become great among you must be your servant, and whoever wants to be first must be your slave—just as the Son of Man did not come to be served, but to serve, and to give his life as a ransom for many" (vv. 26–28).

Yes, Jesus had taught this message of serving before. To be great I must be small—small in my own eyes, humble, putting others first.

Taught by Jesus' example and filled with His love, we are given all power by the Holy Spirit and empowered with Christ Confidence so we can love others through serving others. "For I have given you an example, that you also should do just as I have done to you" (John 13:15 ESV).

He has told us.

When it came to serving in this passage, who did Jesus bypass (v. 12)?

_____

Jesus' holiness never ceases to amaze me! There was not one person that He didn't serve, including His enemy, Judas. Not long after washing the disciples' feet, Jesus dismissed Judas. He could have bypassed Judas by dismissing him *before* He washed their feet. But He didn't.

This night of loving service led up to Jesus giving us all a new commandment: "A new commandment I give to you, that you love one another: just as I have loved you, you also are to love one another. By this all people will know that you are my disciples, if you have love for one another" (13:34–35 ESV).

By *this*. By *love* the world will know we belong to Jesus. By our love for one another the world will come to know True Love.

> ## By our love for one another the world will come to know True Love.

Love is what made the commandment new. Reading the Old Testament, I couldn't say that God's people were primarily known for being loving. Jesus is saying to the disciples, to you and me, "We're doing things differently now."

My *Hebrew-Greek Key Word Study Bible* makes this note: "While the commandment to love was not new (Lev. 19:18, 34), to love in terms demonstrated by the self-sacrifice of Jesus was certainly unprecedented."[40] No one had previously loved to the depth Jesus loved, and no one ever will. He truly is the perfect example. He never told others to do what He had not Himself already done. He even showed love that evening to the very one who would betray Him just a few hours later. What love!

If the world is going to see and know that Jesus is not just another religion but love itself, we are going to have to be people who truly love.

Apply It

How do you and I need to die to ourselves so that others can experience the fullness of life in Christ? In order for others to see His love and want His love in a practical way, what will our loving actions look like?

The people at the coffee shop, the gal in the cubicle beside us, or the neighbors who live next door will not know we are His disciples by our shouting what we stand against. They won't know we are His because of our political stances and social media posts. Jesus clearly tells us there is *one way* for this world to know He is the Way: our loving service for one another.

Open my eyes, Jesus, to see what real love looks like. Please help me die to myself so that You might live in me. In Jesus' name, Amen.

Share in the space below *how* you will love today.

_____

_____

_____

_____

_____

_____

_____

_____

253

★

Parting Words

MEMORY VERSE: "Now, little children, abide in him, so that when he appears we may have confidence and not shrink from him in shame at his coming."—1 John 2:28 (ESV)

SEVERAL YEARS AGO I read a study that resulted in what is called "The Forgetting Curve".[41] This study showed how quickly we forget the things we have read or attempted to learn. We forget the majority (up to 90 percent) of what we read in the first week. (That's not very good news for those of us who are wanting to learn God's Word!) But there is hope! If we review, the rate of forgetfulness declines dramatically! It won't happen on its own though. You must be intentional to retrain your brain to help you remember what God has been saying to you.

That's what we are going to do now. I want you to take a few minutes to look back at our studies in *Fearless Women of the Bible* and, starting on the next page, write several points you learned from these Bible women that have been personal and applicable for you when it comes to finding unshakable confidence.

1. Women of Exodus

_____

_____

_____

_____

2. Daughters of Zelophehad

_____

_____

_____

_____

3. Rahab

_____

_____

_____

_____

4. Deborah

_____

_____

_____

_____

5. Abigail

_____

_____

_____

_____

6. Martha & Mary

_____

_____

_____

Now, take these personal notes and write below one specific action you will take to implement each of these personal takeaways. I'll go first: *I will not stake my confidence on the success of this Bible study. My unshakable confidence is built on my unshakable God, and I will trust Him with it.*

_____

_____

1. Women of Exodus

_____

_____

_____

_____

2. Daughters of Zelophehad

_____

_____

_____

_____

257

3. Rahab

_____

_____

_____

_____

4. Deborah

_____

_____

_____

_____

5. Abigail

_____

_____

_____

_____

6. Martha & Mary

_____

_____

_____

_____

Dinner has wrapped up. Jesus is done washing the disciples' feet and explaining why He did so.

But He's not done yet. He has so much more to say as He prepares His disciples for one thing: His departure.

On this evening, Jesus knew what was ahead. He shares with His disciples that His betrayal would be soon (John 13:21). Just as beside Lazarus's tomb, Jesus is again "troubled in spirit." His anguish is not from a lack of trust. We can feel troubled yet still be fully trusting. His pained heart knew what was to come; He felt the weight of His approaching death and the sorrow of physically leaving His loved ones.

Yet even while He was feeling troubled, Jesus encouraged His disciples.

Digging Deeper

How does Jesus begin this personal time with His disciples? Write out John 14:1 below and circle the actions He calls them to take.

_____

_____

_____

Even when we feel conflicting emotions, Jesus shows us here how we can encourage others. When we speak words of life, our own ears and hearts hear; we are speaking courage to ourselves as well.

The disciples must have also felt conflicting emotions as Jesus spoke of going away to a place they could not come (at least not at the time).

What specific feelings may have stirred inside the disciples when Jesus said, "My Father's house has many rooms; if that were not so, would I have told you that I am going there to prepare a place for you? And if I go and prepare a place for you, I will come back and take you to be with me that you also may be where I am. You know the way to the place where I am going" (John 14:2–4)?

_____

_____

_____

259

When emotions of insecurity want to overwhelm us, we can comfort our hearts with the same truth Jesus gave to His disciples that very night over two thousand years ago:

"I am the way and the truth and the life" (John 14:6). Culture tells us confidence comes with a plan. "Plan your work, then work your plan." We feel empowered when we know where we are going, that is true. Yet peaceful confidence can rest in our hearts even when we don't have a plan, because we know the One with the plan. He is the Way.

Remember back in John 11, when John told us in verse 6 (ESV), "So, when he heard that Lazarus was ill, he stayed two days longer in the place where he was"? Maybe Jesus stalled His coming because Martha, Mary, and Lazarus needed the miracle of Lazarus's resurrection to believe in Christ's resurrection to come? Jesus had told the disciples before they ever left for Bethany: "And for your sake I am glad that I was not there, so that you may believe. But let us go to him" (v. 15). Maybe they needed to see this miracle and the Bethany family had to go through that hard time to prepare all of them for the larger work to which He would be calling them: spreading the gospel to all the world when He was gone.

Friend, this journey you and I are on together is a journey of endurance. It is a journey toward finishing well. Ending well requires us to every day, *day after day*, make the shift: dependence on me to dependence on You, Lord.

How can we finish well this journey of endurance? Read Romans 15:5–6 below and write your thoughts here.

"May the God of endurance and encouragement grant you to live in such harmony with one another, in accord with Christ Jesus, that together you may with one voice glorify the God and Father of our Lord Jesus Christ" (Romans 15:5–6 ESV).

Jesus calls us to begin this journey in Him and to finish firm with Him and in harmony with one another. First Corinthians 1:8 tells us, "He will also keep you firm to the end, so that you will be blameless on the day of our Lord Jesus Christ." He will keep you strong. That is not to say you won't struggle; you will! Yet when you find your confidence wavering and you're shaking, ask yourself: *Where am I drawing my strength from?* This verse begins with the words: He will keep you. Are you allowing Him to do that?

As Jesus prepares to leave the earth to be with the Father, He is setting up His disciples to be confident in who they are and who He is in them. Even though He will no longer be with them physically, He dispels their fears by filling their hearts with powerful promises. These promises were not just for the disciples; they are the promises upon which we will continue to fix our confidence for the rest of our time on earth.

Let's look at these five Christ Commitments for fixing our Confidence:

1. The Promise of Eternal Life

Read John 14:1–4. As Jesus speaks, which of His words encourage you most?

_____

_____

_____

When you and I set our thoughts and focus on eternity, the impact of our fears and failures lessens.

2. The Promise of Answered Prayer

Continue reading John 14:13–14.

I know, that I for one, do not grasp the implications of this promise. "And I will do whatever you ask in my name . . . You may ask me for anything in my name, and I will do it."

What is Jesus' purpose in making such a magnanimous promise to us, so kind and giving?

_____

_____

_____

3. The Promise of the Holy Spirit

Continue with reading John 14:15–18. Why should this promise cause us to feel secure?

_____

_____

_____

This promise, the promise of the Counselor, the Holy Spirit coming to live with us and in us, is one no woman that we have studied so far possessed. We cannot put enough emphasis on the difference having the Holy Spirit residing within you and me makes when it comes to the confidence that can be ours. Every single day when we awake, we have a member of the Godhead living *inside* of us. Guiding us, empowering us, leading us in the way we should go. Because we have such an amazing privilege, we should take full advantage of that power. Communicating with Him and relying on Him for even the smallest parts of our day.

Move down to read verses 25–27, then skip over to John 16:5–16. What does the work of the Holy Spirit in us look like?

_____

_____

4. The Promise of His Peace

Read John 16:33.

His peace will lead us to know when to move, when to wait, and when to get out of His way.

5. The Promise of His Joy

Read John 17:13.

Jesus desires for us to experience His joy in us.

I am so honored that you have chosen to take this journey of finding our unshakable confidence in our unshakable God together with me. It is a trip I needed to take, and I have enjoyed traveling it with you. While you and I are saying good-bye for now, this journey of fixing our confidence in Christ needs to continue until together, we see Him face-to-face.

Let's wrap up this wonderful time we have had together with a prayer that is also our declaration: We will have unshakable confidence in our unshakable God.

Jesus, I admit that I can't do today without You.

Confidence doesn't come naturally to me; it is only something that comes from You. As I rehearse Your faithfulness in my life, my confidence will grow.

There will be times when I have to make my move, even when I don't have the confidence to do it.

When confidence-crushing thoughts overwhelm my mind, guard my mind with the promises in Your Word. My flesh wants to say, "I'm not good enough," but You say, "With Me, all things are possible."

As I walk in Your wisdom and see the blessings that come from obedience, may my faith build in You. And as I wait for Your direction for my next step, help me see when I need to move, wait, or simply get out of Your way.

Enable me to fully understand and live out my spiritual gifts so I can fulfill my calling in Your plan. I know when I am focused on what You have called me to, I can celebrate what You have called others to. Mold me into the confident woman who doesn't have to pull another down in order to pull myself up.

You will ask me to do things beyond my natural abilities. And I'm okay with that because it allows You to do greater things through me than I could ever do alone.

When disappointment and discouragement deplete me, You will restore me.

When life knocks me down, I will choose to draw closer to You still.

I will remember that where You move, the enemy isn't far behind. These trials that come my way are indications that You are at work in my life.

As I take a deep breath in, I feel Your peace from the top of my head to the tips of my toes. And I exhale knowing that with You, I've got the confidence I need for this day.

In Jesus' name, Amen.

Group Discussion Questions

Read this week's memory verse aloud as a group, or select an individual to do so: "Now, little children, abide in him, so that when he appears we may have confidence and not shrink from him in shame at his coming." —1 John 2:28 (ESV)

1. If you've read Mary's story in the past, has the "before" Lazarus's death and "after" of his resurrection difference in Mary ever occurred to you before? How do you explain the impact Jesus' faithfulness had on Mary's confidence?

2. Hebrews 10:35 says, "So do not throw away your confidence; it will be richly rewarded." What are some real-life examples of how we throw away our confidence?

3. You may not have experienced a miracle on the level of your brother rising from the dead, but take a moment to think of a time when you have witnessed God's faithfulness and what that experience did for your confidence in Him. Have one or two share these experiences.

4. After Lazarus rose, Mary humbled herself to anoint Jesus' feet. Explain the correlation between confidence and humility. Is there any area in your life where Jesus would have you humble yourself as you step out in confidence?

5. Finish with these closing questions:

   ▷ The investment of time and energy in this study has been significant. Has it been worth it?

   ▷ What is the most profound thing God has taught you through the *Fearless Women of the Bible*?

   ▷ What have you learned from the women in your group?

   ▷ What have you learned about you?

➤ Is there a next step you feel God compelling you to take? Any unfinished business? Any reconciliation?

Wrap up your time together today by reading the Prayer for Confidence aloud together (pages 263–264). Think of yourself as not only praying the prayer for yourself but also for your sisters in Christ as they continue their journey as well.

Endnotes

1 Warren Baker, ed., *Hebrew-Greek Key Word Study Bible NIV Edition* (Chattanooga: AMG Publishers, 1996).

2 http://www.biblestudytools.com/dictionary/spirit/.

3 http://time.com/3747784/loneliness-mortality/.

4 https://www.biblegateway.com/resources/all-women-bible/Jochebed.

5 http://www.physicsclassroom.com/class/newtlaws/Lesson-1/Newton-s-First -Law.

6 https://en.wikipedia.org/wiki/Harriet_Tubman.

7 https://en.wikipedia.org/wiki/Catherine_Booth.

8 http://www.dictionary.com/browse/confidence?s=t.

9 Baker, ed., *Hebrew-Greek Key Word Study Bible NIV Edition*, 2091.

10 https://www.washingtonpost.com/news/act-four/wp/2016/12/22/hidden -figures-is-terrific-hollywood-could-learn-a-lot-from-it/?utm_term= .98f209fb68ef.

11 Baker, ed., *Hebrew-Greek Key Word Study Bible NIV Edition*, 2118.

12 https://en.wikipedia.org/wiki/Doubt.

13 https://www.biblegateway.com/resources/all-women-bible/Rahab.

14 Wendy Blight, *I Know His Name* (Nashville: Thomas Nelson: 2015).

15 http://www.chabad.org/library/article_cdo/aid/112050/jewish/The -Prophetess-Deborah.htm.

16 Baker, ed., *Hebrew-Greek Key Word Study Bible NIV Edition*, 2115.

17 http://www.sacred-texts.com/bib/cmt/henry/jdg004.htm.

18 http://www.dictionary.com/browse/confidence?s=t.

19 http://www.thequotablecoach.com/teach-your-daughters-to-worry/.

20 http://biblehub.com/commentaries/judges/4-17.htm.

21 Ibid.

22 Baker, ed., *Hebrew-Greek Key Word Study Bible NIV Edition*, 1982.

23 Ibid., 1906.

24 Ibid., 1534.

25 Ibid., 2014.

26 http://biblehub.com/commentaries/2_samuel/6-14.htm.

27 http://www.dictionary.com/browse/despise?s=t.

28 Baker, ed., *Hebrew-Greek Key Word Study Bible NIV Edition*, 1921.

29 Ibid., 1943.

30 http://biblehub.com/hebrew/3045.htm.

31 https://www.facebook.com/OfficialLysa/photos/a.427520367693.211047.338
478917693/10152410084557694/?type=1&theater.

32 Baker, ed., *Hebrew-Greek Key Word Study Bible NIV Edition*, 2014.

33 Ibid., 1962.

34 Rebecca St. James, *Sister Freaks: Stories of Women Who Gave Up Everything for God* (New York: Warner Faith, 2005), 5.

35 http://www.religioustolerance.org/ofe_bibl.htm.

36 Baker, ed., *Hebrew-Greek Key Word Study Bible NIV Edition*, 1063.

37 https://www.biblegateway.com/resources/all-women-bible/Martha.

38 Baker, ed., *Hebrew-Greek Key Word Study Bible NIV Edition*, 2011.

39 http://www.biblestudytools.com/dictionary/anointing/.

40 Baker, ed., *Hebrew-Greek Key Word Study Bible NIV Edition*, 1635.

41 https://sidsavara.com/personal-productivity/the-ebbinghaus-curve-of
-forgetting.

About the Author

Lynn Cowell is a national conference speaker who passionately empowers women of all ages to understand the importance of Christ confidence. She is the author of several books including *Esther: Seeing Our Invisible God in an Uncertain World* and *Loved and Cherished* just for girls ages 8–12. Lynn also serves on the speaking and writing teams for Proverbs 31 Ministries.

Website: If you enjoyed *Fearless Women of the Bible*, you can find additional empowering resources at www.LynnCowell.com and www.Proverbs31.org.

Connect with Lynn, see pictures of her family, and find out where you can meet in person at her speaking events:

Blog: www.LynnCowell.com
Facebook: www.Facebook.com/lynn.m.cowell
Instagram: @LynnCowell
Twitter: @LynnCowell

Proverbs 31 Ministries

If you were inspired by Lynn Cowell or *Fearless Women of the Bible* and desire to deepen your own personal relationship with Jesus Christ, we encourage you to connect with Proverbs 31 Ministries.

Proverbs 31 Ministries exists to help you know the truth and live the truth, for it changes everything. We come alongside you through:

- ➤ Free online daily devotions
- ➤ First 5 Bible study app
- ➤ Daily radio program
- ➤ Books and resources
- ➤ Online Bible Studies
- ➤ COMPEL Writers Training: www.CompelTraining.com
- ➤ Speakers for events

To learn more about Proverbs 31 Ministries, call 877-731-4663 or visit www.Proverbs31.org.

Proverbs 31 Ministries
PO Box 3189
Matthews, NC 28106
www.Proverbs31.org

A Prayer for Confidence

Jesus, I admit that I can't do today without You.

Confidence doesn't come naturally to me; it is only something that comes from You. As I rehearse Your faithfulness in my life, my confidence will grow.

There will be times when I have to make my move, even when I don't have the confidence to do it.

When confidence-crushing thoughts overwhelm my mind, guard my mind with the promises in Your Word. My flesh wants to say, "I'm not good enough," but You say, "With Me, all things are possible."

As I walk in Your wisdom and see the blessings that come from obedience, may my faith build in You. And as I wait for Your direction for my next step, help me see when I need to move, wait, or simply get out of Your way.

Enable me to fully understand and live out my spiritual gifts so I can fulfill my calling in Your plan. I know when I am focused on what You have called me to, I can celebrate what You have called others to. Mold me into the confident woman who doesn't have to pull another down in order to pull myself up.

You will ask me to do things beyond my natural abilities. And I'm okay with that because it allows You to do greater things through me than I could ever do alone.

When disappointment and discouragement deplete me, You will restore me.

When life knocks me down, I will choose to draw closer to You still.

I will remember that where You move, the enemy isn't far behind. These trials that come my way are indications that You are at work in my life.

As I take a deep breath in, I feel Your peace from the top of my head to the tips of my toes. And I exhale knowing that with You, I've got the confidence I need for this day.

In Jesus' name, Amen.